CHARLOTTE AVERY ON ISLE ROYALE

by Rebecca S. Curtis

Illustrated by Catherine Baer

Midwest Traditions, Inc.
Mount Horeb, Wisconsin
1995

Midwest Traditions, Inc. is a nonprofit educational organization devoted to the study and preservation of the folk history and traditional cultures of the American Midwest. Our publications serve to bring this rich, diverse heritage to broader public attention.

For a catalog of books and other materials, write:
Midwest Traditions
PO Box 320
Mount Horeb, Wisconsin 53572 USA
(telephone 1-800-736-9189)

Manufactured in the United States of America
Printed on acid-free paper

Book Design: Lisa Teach-Swaziek, PeachTree Design
Editor: Jean M. Johnson

Publisher's Cataloging-in-Publication Data
Curtis, Rebecca S.
     Charlotte Avery on Isle Royale / by Rebecca S. Curtis;
illustrated by Catherine Baer.
          p. cm.
     Summary: Young Charlotte and her family spend a year in the 1870s on Isle Royale in Lake Superior, discovering its natural beauty and folk history through adventures with local characters and friends.
     Library of Congress Catalog Card # 95-75504
     ISBN 1-883953-09-X (hc), ISBN 1-883953-13-8 (pb)
     1. Frontier and pioneer life – Middle West – Fiction. 2. Natural history – Isle Royale (Mich.) – Fiction. I. Baer, Catherine, ill. II. Title.
PS3553.W123C43 1995   813'.54
                                                        QBI95-20061

First Paperback Edition
10 9 8 7 6 5 5 3 2

For James,
who was my best friend
long before he became
my husband.

TABLE OF CONTENTS

CHAPTER 1

FIRE IN CHICAGO

"READY OR NOT, here I come!" Charlotte Avery let her hands drop from her eyes and silently scanned the schoolyard. "I like it much better when I'm the one hiding," she thought to herself, as she absently peered down into the dark, empty rain barrel. She had thought she might find Molly there. Since the rain stopped falling, this had become one of the favored hiding places. Molly was the littlest girl in school, and Charlotte always found her first, usually somewhere quite close to the front door. Small puffs of dust clouded around Charlotte's shoes as she turned toward the schoolhouse. She brushed a loose strand of hair from her face. It was a warm day for Chicago in October. She bent over and peered under the steps. Molly smiled brightly and Charlotte grabbed her small hand.

"Now you can help me find the others," said Charlotte. She squatted down in the dust and picked up a beetle that was on its back, frantically waving legs in the air. The beetle, now righted, trundled off on its business, leaving tiny poofs of dust in its wake.

Molly pulled Charlotte to a clump of bushes and they crouched down to look underneath. The shout came so suddenly that Charlotte jerked quickly, caught her foot on a root, and sat down hard.

"Fire!" The shout came from Robin, Charlotte's fourteen-year-old brother. He looked toward the west and pointed. "The hotel is on fire, and so is the livery next to it!" The other children scrambled out from their hiding places and stared at the billowing clouds of dark smoke.

"That's not all, Rob!" cried Charlotte, fear in her eyes. "Look beyond that! It looks like the whole city is starting to burn!" There was a small sniffle beside her, and Charlotte glanced down at Molly.

"I'm scared," she whimpered in a trembling voice. Charlotte pulled her handkerchief from her pocket and dabbed at Molly's tear-stained cheeks.

"Don't cry, Molly. Teacher will know what to do."

But her own voice trembled and she moved close to Robin. He began barking orders, "Henry Jacobs, go and fetch Teacher. Hurry! The rest of you gather round now." They gathered about Robin, holding hands tightly, all the while staring at the streams of dark smoke and the giant tongues of orange and red flames which devoured every wooden structure in the distance.

The teacher burst into action with one look at the flames spreading across the city. Lifting her skirts, she ran to the frightened huddle of children.

"Quickly children, join hands with a partner. We must get away from here—toward the lake! Stay behind me now!" She grabbed little Molly's hand and Charlotte clung desperately to Robin. He was trying to be brave, but Charlotte could see fear in his eyes.

Charlotte felt hot tears running down her cheeks as she ran surrounded by silent, terror-stricken faces. "Robin will take care of me," she whispered to herself, as she gulped in air breathlessly. She thought of home. Home—where Papa would be sitting at the table eating Mama's good hot lunch. And after lunch Papa would hold five-year-old William on his knee and tell him stories about England. England was far away across the Atlantic Ocean. Charlotte was born there, as well as Robin, and of course Mama and Papa. But Charlotte didn't remember England. She had been only two years old when they came to America. Robin remembered things, though—walks in a lovely green park, musicians on a street corner, nibbling on hot roasted chestnuts on a bench beside the river Thames.

With a start, she pulled her jumbled thoughts back to the present. Everyone in the neighborhood seemed to be running for their lives. A slender woman in a billowy flowered dress clutched a screaming child by the hand. An old man with a great flowing beard carried a clock in a walnut case. A young woman clutched a velvet-covered photograph album to her chest as she ran, wiping at tears that blurred her vision.

"What's happening?" Robin yelled to no one as they continued running. "All of Chicago must be on fire!" The fear in his eyes had turned to terror, but still he clutched Charlotte's sweaty hand and they ran on. Charlotte felt the heat from the flames behind her. It seemed that a giant hot wind pushed them forward endlessly.

They ran until she thought her heart would burst, and then just ahead she saw the blue, sparkling water of Lake Michigan. When they reached the shore, she fell to her knees in the sand, heaving for breath, as tears of relief wet her eyes. Finally, when she could speak again, she lifted her head and looked at Robin, who sprawled on the sand beside her. Together, their eyes opened wide at the scene of horror behind them. Chicago was an inferno. Red and yellow flames towered up in the sky, devouring every wooden structure in their relentless path. In their wake they left charred, smoldering skeletons that crumbled into ashes and fell to the ground. Charlotte strained to hear Teacher's voice above the roaring, wailing crowd.

"Children! Further! We must go further into the water! I know it's cold, but I think we will be safe there!"

Charlotte gasped as the chill October water of the lake lapped over the tops of her leather shoes. She thought, "What will Mama say when she sees that I have ruined my school shoes?" Then she wailed out loud, "Mama and Papa, I need you!" Her cries joined with those around her and Robin stood beside her, one arm protectively around her shoulders. Real fear gripped her heart and she could not stop the flow of salty tears that fell from her cheeks like raindrops on the water—like tiny sprinkles at the beginning of a storm.

Swarms of people milled about in the freezing water, shocked and disoriented. Charlotte watched as a woman in a faded calico dress lunged toward the protecting water of the lake. In one arm she held a crying baby. The other hand tightly gripped the hand of a toddler. A third child, a boy, followed a short distance behind. The woman's glance turned to concern and then to dismay as the young child, walking alone, stopped and gazed at the flames in fascination. The helpless mother watched, terrified, as the boy turned in confused circles and then headed back toward the blazing buildings.

Charlotte tore free from Robin's grasp and ran toward the child. She reached the boy and grabbed his hand, tugging his unwilling body toward the water. His mother gratefully met them, shouting at the child in anger and relief.

Charlotte opened her mouth to speak to the woman, but before the words could come out, she felt a great blow from behind, saw a jumble of wheels and horses and legs, and winced at a sudden explosive pain in one leg. Something hit her hard in the head. And the world went black.

CHAPTER 2

AFTER THE FIRE

SUNSHINE POURED THROUGH the open window and a gentle breeze lifted the white starched curtains. A pot of Mama's cheery red geraniums rested on the stand beside the bed. Papa sat in the high-backed rocking chair pushed close to the bed. His eyes twinkled as Charlotte's eyes fluttered open and she stared at him, confused.

"Papa! You're here, and I'm here too! We're home! What happened? The fire—so much smoke and so many people. I couldn't find you and Mama! I tried to help a little boy and... Ow! My leg! What happened to my leg? It hurts, Papa!"

Two large tears squeezed out and rolled down her cheeks. She brushed them away and felt ashamed. She was ten years old—too old to cry—but it seemed that she couldn't stop the tears.

Papa picked up her hand and smoothed the damp hair from her forehead.

"Don't cry anymore, little Charli. A lot of men are working very hard to put the fires out. Most of it is under control already. Mama is fine and so are William and Robin. We're all home together now and you don't need to fret anymore. You are a fine, brave girl, Charli, and Mama and I are proud of you! You saved that little boy's life, you know. His mother will never forget you. She was here this morning, but I wouldn't let her wake you."

Charlotte listened carefully and then asked, "What about my leg, Papa? Why does it hurt so?"

"It hurts because it's broken," he answered solemnly. "A run-away team of horses with a wagon bumped you from behind and knocked you right over. Your leg got twisted under you when you fell. You bumped your head, and you've been asleep all night."

"Did I bleed, Papa?" Charlotte had stopped crying and looked with interest at the wooden splints on her leg.

"No, Charli. You didn't bleed at all. We were lucky to find a doctor to put a splint on your leg so quickly. But there won't be much hide-and-seek for you for the next few weeks!"

"That's right, Charlotte. You're to stay right there in

bed for the next three weeks. After that the doctor says you can try a crutch." Mama set down the breakfast tray and leaned over to put a light kiss on Charlotte's cheek. "We've had an anxious night waiting for you to wake up." Then her lips trembled and she quickly brushed away a tear. Papa put an arm firmly around Mama's waist.

"Well, well, let's be done with tears for now! All's well that ends well. Now Charli must have her breakfast!"

Charlotte sniffed the tray and suddenly realized that she was starving. A thin wisp of steam rose from the bowl of porridge. There were fried potatoes and a wedge of apple pie with a piece of yellow cheese melting down its sides.

The porridge slid smoothly down her throat. The last bite of pie was raised to her lips, when a small golden-haired head peeped up from the edge of the bed and two chubby arms encircled her neck.

"William!" she laughed, and picked up the smear of pie that had fallen on her night-dress. "I'm so glad to see you. And here is Rob, too. Come in, big brother! I want all of my family with me."

Robin came slowly across the room and touched her arm shyly. His voice quivered when he spoke. "Are you mad at me, Charli? I tried to protect you, but everything happened so fast! I didn't even see the wagon until it was too late." He dropped his head and mumbled, "It's my fault about your broken leg."

Charlotte grasped his hands firmly. "You were wonderful, Rob. You *did* take care of me, and the other children, too. I never could have run so far without you there beside me, holding me up."

Robin looked at the floor, embarrassed, but his strained features relaxed a bit.

"All right, everybody," announced Mama. "Charlotte has had enough excitement for now. Time for her to get some rest."

Papa paused for a moment and tucked the soft coverlet around her chin. "I love you, my little Charli," he whispered softly.

"I love you too, Papa," she said contentedly, and snuggled down into the feather bed with a deep sigh.

In the kitchen, Mama set the china teapot on the carved wooden table and brought down two cups from the cupboard. She poured out the tea and sat down across from Papa. A worried look flitted across her face.

"What shall we do, Ian? I am so thankful that we are all safe and our home was spared, but there are many people in Chicago who aren't so fortunate. They've lost everything—homes, businesses, and loved ones. My heart just aches for them."

Papa took a sip of tea and looked gravely into her eyes. "There is terrible suffering in this city and we must help. There will need to be temporary shelters built for those who have lost their homes. With my construction experience, I can help with that."

Mama nodded in agreement, as she cut thin slices of fruit cake. Papa continued. "But I have another idea, as well. With this large house we have plenty of room for an extra family, if we take the furniture out of the parlor and put the boys together in one bedroom for awhile.

"I know you have Charlotte to look after now, and this would mean even more work..."

Mama interrupted abruptly. "It's a wonderful idea, Ian. And you are a dear to think of it. No man has a kinder heart."

Papa pushed his chair back and pulled on his jacket. "It's settled then," he stated as he pulled Mama close. "I'll go out and join the work crews. With Rob's help, we can have the parlor ready for a family by tonight." He kissed her quickly and pulled the wooden door shut behind him.

CHAPTER 3

PAPA MAKES A DECISION

THE NEXT EIGHT WEEKS were the busiest the Avery family had ever known. Papa worked long, hard days helping to build temporary structures for those who had lost homes in the terrible fire. The final count, Papa told them, came to 17,000 buildings destroyed, 300 lives lost, and 90,000 people left homeless. Papa's skills as an architect and carpenter were in great demand. He had been trained for many years as a young man in England. But Chicago was full of young eager folks from all parts of Europe, and they worked with great energy to rebuild the city. By the end of the first week after the fire, 6,000 temporary shelters had been constructed.

Mama worked from sunrise to sunset cooking, cleaning, and washing laundry for her own family, as well as the steady stream of house guests who came and left every few days. Robin fetched wood, built fires in the cook stove, pumped water, and lifted endless tubs of wet laundry. He sometimes grumbled about doing "women's work," but an occasional stern look from Mama silenced him quickly.

It was a trying time for Charlotte, who was accustomed to days of endless activity. Her leg was mending nicely, but Mama still wouldn't let her out of bed for more than a slow hobble about the house once a day. She longed to help out with the housework, but Mama was firm.

"Charlotte, you are getting better, I know, but you mind the doctor and stay put. You'll be up and about soon enough." So Charlotte would sigh and work on a bit of mending, or read from her books of poetry. She didn't need two strong legs to mind William, though. He had never had his sister to himself for so long and could not be persuaded to leave her room. He played with tiddly-winks at the foot of her bed and begged for stories.

"Charli," William said in a serious voice one snowy afternoon, "when your leg gets all better, will you still play with me? I wish I could always be with you." His blue eyes looked at her steadily.

Charlotte fluffed his golden curls. "You are my only little brother, Will. I love to have you here with me.

You make me happy—this bedroom would be an awfully lonesome place without your company." That brought his smile back and he jumped up happily, scattering tiddly-winks to far corners of the polished floor.

By the end of the year, the residents of Chicago had found housing for most of the homeless, and Mama and Robin wearily pushed the heavy sofa and wing chairs back into the parlor.

Snow stood in deep drifts outside, but in the house, preparations were made for a festive New Year's dinner.

Charlotte walked with only the slightest limp, and on New Year's Day she carefully set the table with Mama's best china and silverware. The kitchen was full of wonderful smells: roast turkey with onion dressing, mashed potatoes and gravy, yellow buttered squash, fresh brown bread, and several kinds of preserves.

When the family gathered at the large table, Charlotte sat between Papa and William. Papa's prayer was a long one. He gave thanks for the bounty of food and for the warm, comfortable house. He thanked God for a good year in 1871, and for the new year ahead. Charlotte's stomach rumbled and she peeked at the two pies she had helped Mama prepare. Her mouth watered for a piece of pumpkin pie. She gulped hard, shut her eyes again, and tried to concentrate on Papa's prayer. When at last her plate was loaded, she ate heartily. As Mama began serving coffee and tea, Papa noisily cleared his throat.

"I have something to say to all of you," he began, choosing words slowly and deliberately. "You have all worked hard these past few months and I am proud of each of you. Despite the terrible fire, God has taken care of us in 1871. I am certain that 1872 will be better." He paused for a moment and fidgeted nervously with his napkin.

"I received a letter last week from a mining company in Michigan. It seems that this company has recently begun a mining operation on an island in Lake Superior, and they are in need of an architect. I was offered the position of chief architect and carpenter at the new mine site. Your Mama and I have come to the decision that this is an exciting opportunity for our family.

"We feel that now is a good time for all of us to make a fresh start in a new place. We will leave Chicago in May to begin the journey to the far north, in time for me to take the boat to the island on the first of June."

Robin, Charlotte, and William had all stopped eating their dessert, and stared at Papa in amazement. At last Robin found his voice.

"What is this island called, Papa?"

"It's called Isle Royale," Papa replied.

CHAPTER 4

THE JOURNEY

May 15, 1872

Papa says that this trip is one I'll always want to remember, so I'm going to keep a diary as we make our journey from Chicago to Isle Royale.

It is just past 10:00 p.m. and we are on board the steam ship *Peerless* bound for Grand Haven, Michigan. We departed from Milwaukee just an hour ago. How happy I am to finally be on our way!

Mama and Papa talked for a long time about how we should make the long journey. Everyone in the family had different ideas. Mama, who gets frightfully seasick, favored driving a wagon straight north through Wisconsin and into Michigan. Papa said that would take too long, and with the rough roads we might lose a wagon wheel or get lost along the way. Robin couldn't quit talking about ships. He spent hours poring over books and maps of the Great Lakes. He said the fastest way to reach Isle Royale is by ship from Chicago up Lake Michigan to the Straits of Mackinac, then through the locks at Sault Sainte Marie, and west across Lake Superior.

William, who hasn't put down his new toy train since Christmas, wants to ride a train all the way to the island. I explained to him that Isle Royale is surrounded by water. We couldn't possibly ride the train all the way there. I'm not sure he believed me. For my part, I was so thrilled with the idea of a great adventure, I didn't care how we went—I only wished that we would get started!

It turned out that Papa's new boss made the decision for us. The owner of the mine wants Papa to go to Detroit first to look over plans for the mine and order lumber. So we took the train from Chicago to Milwaukee, and are riding on a ship across Lake Michigan to Grand Haven. There we will take another train to Detroit. Then, we'll take boats the rest of the way to Isle Royale.

I've been writing for awhile and Mama says I must put out the light so we can all get some sleep. In the morning we'll be in Grand Haven and I'll have my first look at Michigan. I don't think I'll be able to sleep a wink tonight!

May 18, 1872

There is so much to see and do that I simply can't find time to write in my diary every day.

The port of Grand Haven was small and very different from Chicago! It had several churches, lots of shops, and one hotel. Mama and Papa rushed us right from the boat to the train, so I had no time at all to explore.

The train was great fun! There were passenger cars as well as freight cars, and plenty of room to roam about. The seats were soft and springy and covered with dark red velvet. There were sitting cars, sleeping cars, and a dining car.

It took only a couple of hours to reach the inland town of Grand Rapids, and here we got off the train and made our way to the National Hotel. Papa has a friend in Grand Rapids who owns the Widdicomb Brothers Furniture Company. Papa wanted to visit his friend and let Mama order some new furniture.

Grand Rapids is a fun place to explore. This city is known for logging as well as making furniture. The logs are floated downstream on the Grand River, which runs through the center of town. Sometimes when there are a great many logs in the river at once, there is a terrific jam and lots of people come out of stores and offices to watch the excitement.

Last night we had dinner at a restaurant called the Cosmopolitan. Papa said we might order dessert, so we each had a dish of ice cream. What a delicious special treat! After dinner I saw some lovely dress material in a store front and pointed it out to Mama. She said that we'll do a bit of shopping when we reach Detroit. Papa says Detroit is the largest city in Michigan. I wonder if it's like Chicago. I can't wait to see it!

Will is jumping up and down and pointing at the train as it rumbles up to the station. I must go for now. Goodbye to Grand Rapids!

May 21, 1872

We have been in Detroit for three days and it has been such fun!

The train ride from Grand Rapids took about nine hours. Papa said that we traveled around twenty miles per hour! We made many stops in towns along the way to load and unload passengers and freight.

We are staying at a fine hotel called the Biddle House. It has enough rooms for 500 guests and costs three dollars a day! Papa's boss is paying for our rooms, as well as meals which we take in an enormous dining room.

Papa spends a great deal of time at the mine office going over plans and figures and lumber orders. Yesterday he took Rob and Will with him, so Mama

and I spent the whole day together.

We ate lunch at a sidewalk cafe and Mama let me order an Italian ice for dessert. Rob and Will will be so jealous when I tell them!

There are a great many interesting shops selling everything from shoes to wicker furniture. Mama bought three cases of groceries and enough dress fabric to make both of us two new dresses. She says it's best to be prepared since we don't know what is available on the island.

On the way back to the hotel we stopped at a bookstore and Mama said I could choose a book to read on the ship. I picked out one called *Swiss Family Robinson*. It's a story about a family living on an island and it looks like it is full of exciting adventures!

May 24, 1872

It will take us about eight days on the steam ship *Winslow* to travel from Detroit to Copper Harbor, Michigan! So far the trip has been very interesting with lots of changing scenery.

When we left Detroit, the harbor was a very busy place, full of steam boats and sailing vessels all unloading freight and passengers. It took two days to cross Lake St. Clair and go up the St. Clair River. It was cloudy and rainy when we passed Port Huron and Fort Gratiot, and the river opened up to Lake Huron.

We steamed up Lake Huron for three more days. As we headed north, Michigan's shore was in sight most of the way, but to the north nothing was visible but water. The lake was pretty calm. Mama even came up on deck to watch the passing ships. At the Soo Locks, we rode up the St. Mary's River to finally get our first glimpse of Lake Superior. It was dramatic to see the American flag, the Stars and Stripes, flying over Fort Brady and across the river, Canada's colorful Red Ensign fluttering over the Canadian shore.

May 28, 1872

We've almost made it to Isle Royale! It's so wild and exciting on Lake Superior!

It took another four days on Lake Superior to reach Copper Harbor. We followed the south shoreline. Sunset over the lake is the most beautiful I've ever seen. Chicago seems a million miles away! As we headed west we saw big sand dunes and the wonderful cliffs called Pictured Rocks from the ship. We stopped in Marquette which is a very busy port with many steamers arriving and departing daily. Lots of people come here for health reasons. The air is so fresh!

On our last day on the *Winslow* we made a 95-mile voyage from Marquette to Copper Harbor through the night. This is a small mining town way up north on a peninsula called the Keweenaw. This peninsula is as beautiful as can be! The woods are full of evergreens, the sky is deep blue, and the air pure and clean.

Papa will leave for Isle Royale right away and we will join him in a week. He seems very excited.

Papa was right about keeping this little journal. It was lots of fun. I am looking forward to writing down my next great adventure. Maybe some day I'll be a great author like Johann Wyss—the man who wrote *Swiss Family Robinson!*

Fairy Slipper

CHAPTER 5

ARRIVAL ON ISLE ROYALE

THE HARBOR LAY SHROUDED in thick white fog as the boat pulled away from the dock in Copper Harbor. A family of Canada geese swam by serenely, taking no notice of the activity inside the large vessel. A beam of light from the lighthouse pierced through the fog at regular intervals. From the dock came cries of gulls, swooping down to grasp remains of yesterday's picnic lunch.

Charlotte leaned over the boat's railing and gazed down into the deep-green water. Where it was shallow she could see large, moss-covered rocks on the bottom. The sudden bellow of the ship's horn caused her to jump. Robin chuckled beside her.

"Scared you, didn't it, Charli? Here," he said handing her a thick muffler and heavy woolen mittens. "Mama says you have to wear these."

Charlotte grunted in disgust, "I'm not cold and I'm not a baby and you can't..."

Mama stepped between them, pulled the muffler from Charlotte's hands and wrapped it firmly around her head, over her ears, and tied it securely under her defiant chin.

"You will keep this on, and the mittens too, as long as you insist on being outside. It gets cold on the lake, and I won't have you sniffling and sneezing before we even reach the island. Now mind me, Charlotte."

Charlotte sighed and pulled on the red and white striped mittens. She knew that to protest further would be futile. When Mama's mouth was set in that firm line, she meant to be obeyed.

The boat was soon out of the harbor and into open Lake Superior. When Charlotte looked back, Copper Harbor had already been swallowed up in the fog. She breathed in deeply and raised her face to the sky, her eyes closed.

"I think I love Lake Superior already," she said to herself. She looked down when she heard a small giggle.

"How do you know that, Charli?" asked William. "I can't even see the lake. Will the fog go away before we get to Isle Royale?"

Charlotte grasped his mittened hand in hers. "I don't know about the fog, Will, but it's kind of nice like this, too, isn't it? It's like being in the center of a giant white cocoon. We can pretend we're caterpillars trying to break free and become butterflies."

William laughed again. "You always have funny ideas, Charli. Why doesn't Mama stay on deck to look at the fog? She just lies down and her face is all whitish."

"Mama doesn't like to be on the water," replied Charlotte. "She gets seasick, so you'd best not bother her. I'm so glad she lets us be outside though, aren't you? You can stay right here with me. I see that Rob has already made friends with the captain. He'll probably spend all his time in the wheelhouse, asking questions about engines and steam and foghorns and navigation."

The air was chilly. William snuggled closer to Charlotte and slipped one of his hands into her coat pocket.

Lunch tasted good at noon. Mama had bought it in Copper Harbor and there was plenty. The cold fried chicken was tender and juicy. There were biscuits with butter and honey, shiny red apples, twisted sugared donuts, and a jar of fresh milk, still cool from the ice box.

They were finishing the last of the donuts, when

Charlotte sprang suddenly to her feet and pointed out the window.

"Look, look! The fog is clearing away! I couldn't see that far out before, and look, there are birds following behind the boat!" She nearly knocked over her glass of milk in her excitement.

"Yes, Charlotte," Mama said. "We must be getting closer to land, but mercy on us, must you startle us so? Sit down and finish your milk."

Charlotte sat back down and finished her half glass of milk in three giant swallows. She bolted out the door and Mama shook her head as she picked up the remains of their lunch.

On deck the scene was changing dramatically. The white curtain of fog had lifted to reveal the shining blue water as far as the eye could see. Charlotte looked hard in all directions, but couldn't see any land at all. She could see the line that was formed where the water met the sky, but there was nothing to break that line. She leaned over the rail and peered into the water. She tried to decide what color it was, but finally realized that she knew no name to describe it—it was blue and green and gray all mixed together. The water near the boat churned and foamed. It gathered in millions of tiny bubbles that fizzled beneath the surface, and then suddenly came bursting to the top in white foam. It danced all about, churning and mixing and bubbling. Charlotte watched until the endless spirals of water began to make her dizzy.

She sat down on a bench and breathed a sigh of contentment. The lake made her feel wild and free and full of adventure.

When land came into view, it first appeared to be nothing more than a mass of low-lying clouds in the horizon. But as the boat drew nearer, the shapes began to lengthen and define. The trees stood tall and proud and covered the island in a great forest. There were pine trees and spruce and birch and aspen. Some of them seemed to grow right out of the craggy rocks that hugged the shoreline. The massive rocks were colorful in the sunshine, covered with patches of orange and green and white lichen. Hairy moss hung heavily from the tree branches and grew thickly on their bark. The white bark of birch and aspen made a strong contrast to the dark green backdrop of evergreens.

Mama came up on deck. Her cheeks soon lost their pale whiteness. "Look children," she said quietly. "We have reached Isle Royale at last. Look long and remember what you see. You will always want to remember when you first saw this place."

"Isle Royale isn't alone," Charlotte observed. "There are lots of other little islands about."

Robin piped up. "The captain told me that there are about two hundred islands that make up what people call Isle Royale. It's called an archipelago and..."

Charlotte interrupted his speech with a squeal of excitement. "There's the dock and I think I see Papa! Yes, he's waving!"

They waved eagerly as the great boat pulled alongside the broad dock. Strong arms of crew members threw heavy ropes out onto the dock where they were caught and tied around short cleats making the boat fast.

Charlotte was the first to reach Papa, but she staggered a bit, her legs wobbly as she ran into his outstretched arms.

"Careful, Charli," he laughed as he hugged her strongly. "You haven't got your land legs yet!" Then he rumpled Robin's dark hair and swung William up on his shoulders.

"How did you like your boat ride, little man?"

"Oh Papa!" William cried. "We saw fog and big white birds with yellow beaks, and so much water all around. And Rob says this is an archipel-archipel..."

"Rob was right," said Papa. "Only it's pronounced, archi-*pel*-ago. It means a large group of islands. Isle Royale is the largest of the group. It's forty-five miles long and about nine miles wide."

He set William down on the dock and took one of Mama's small hands in his large ones. He gently raised it to his lips. Mama glanced about, embarrassed but pleased. "Oh Ian," she said, "we have all missed you so much! It is good that we are all together again!"

Papa's eyes twinkled as he led them toward a waiting wagon. "I think you'll like the house, Elizabeth. Come along Charli, there will be plenty of time for exploring. And there is someone at the village who is anxious to meet you."

Charlotte tugged on Papa's sleeve. "Could this 'someone' be a girl my age, Papa? Is she nice? Is her hair dark like mine? What will I say to her? Do you think she will like me?" Charlotte fiddled nervously with the large buttons on her coat.

"Mercy on us, child!" said Mama. "You will know soon enough. Be still now, Charlotte. Will has fallen asleep. The nap will do him good."

So Charlotte held her tongue. But she couldn't stop thinking about the new girl. Maybe they would become best friends. The thought made her feel all trembly inside.

On the front wagon seat, two men spoke to Mama. One of them was Michael Cadieu, the manager of the mine and Papa's boss. They told Mama about the village of Island Mine as the wagon rolled along the bumpy road. A team of huge matched Percheron horses pulled the heavy wagon.

"It's about three and a half miles from the dock here at Siskiwit Bay to Island Mine," said Mr. Cadieu's assistant. "You'll find that the dry goods store has about anything you could want. And of course there's the church that doubles as a school. We'll be getting a new teacher this fall, I understand."

Mama looked pleased. "We didn't really know what to expect, so I brought a lot of supplies with us. But it's nice to know that we won't be living in a complete wilderness."

Robin had been listening quietly to the conversation and asked, "Is there a job for me, Papa? I'll be fifteen soon and I'm pretty strong, you know."

Mr. Cadieu looked at Robin with interest. "I could use a good bellows boy down at the mine. You look like you could handle that fine, son."

Robin's eyes shone and he looked at Papa, pleading, "Could I, Papa, please? I would still have time for chores in the morning."

"Yes, Rob," replied Papa thoughtfully. "Your Mama and I had discussed the possibility. We think it would be a good experience for you, but only during the summer. When September rolls around you'll go to school with the other children."

"Yes, Papa," said Robin. His smile lit up his whole face.

The wagon rounded a bend and the small village of Island Mine sprang up before them. The rough dirt road that was Main Street had on one side a black-smith shop, dry goods store, and several tiny log homes. On the other side was a large building with two stories where many miners lived. They turned off Main Street and pulled up to a large, white-painted house. Tall maple trees stood around it and rope with a wooden seat hung from one of the branches.

Charlotte jumped from the wagon and was startled to find someone there. She stared. She had never seen such red hair. "She must have a thousand freckles," Charlotte thought to herself.

"Charlotte, I'd like you to meet my daughter, Claire," Mr. Cadieu said. "I think the two of you might be in the same class this fall."

"Hello. How old are you?" said Charlotte timidly. "I'm ten."

"I turned eleven last month," Claire replied softly. "But Gram says I'm small for my age. Here, I picked this for you."

She held out the prettiest, most delicate flower Charlotte had ever seen. It had a thin, fragile stem with a blossom shaped just like a tiny slipper. Five slender spikes pointed from the top. Charlotte touched it softly.

"I've never seen anything so lovely," she whispered. What is it called?"

"It's called Calypso, or fairy slipper. I know where there are lots of them. Come on, I'll show you!" She grabbed Charlotte's hand and they ran toward a footpath among the maple trees.

CHAPTER 6

GETTING SETTLED

MAMA WAS PLEASED with the large, white-painted house. There were two floors, with a cellar underneath. The cellar was cool and dry. It had long wooden shelves to hold canned goods, wooden barrels to hold fresh vegetables, and pegs nailed into the wall where smoked meats could hang. On the first floor there were four large rooms. The kitchen was light and cheery, with wooden cupboards, a table, and a stove for cooking. It opened into the dining room, which held the long dining table and six sturdy chairs. The parlor was a pleasant, comfortable place to relax and read or visit, with soft cozy chairs and a large stone fireplace.

Papa's office occupied the other room. In it stood a large desk and cupboards in which to store supplies. A narrow stairway led to three bedrooms upstairs. The largest was Mama and Papa's. Robin and William would share a room, and the other one was just the right size for Charlotte.

Mama walked through with William tagging along behind. The house would be quite suitable when her fine pictures were hung and the furniture put in place. But she would need Charlotte's help. She went to the front door and called "Charlotte!" in a loud voice. It took three tries before Charlotte appeared, breathless and excited.

"Oh Mama," she cried. "Have you ever dreamed of anyplace as lovely as this? That girl is Claire Cadieu and she has the reddest hair you ever saw and so many freckles! She is just three months older than me, but she has been here for a year with her father and grandma. But she doesn't call her Grandma; she calls her Gram. Isn't that funny? She gave me the prettiest flower, see? It's called fairy slipper and I know where to find lots of them now. But Claire says we mustn't pick a great many. They look so pretty in the forest." She paused to catch her breath and Mama interrupted quickly.

"The flower is lovely, Charli, and I'm glad you found a friend. You will have lots of time to get to know each other. Right now I need your help in the house." She smiled at her only daughter and pulled a twig from her hair. "Change your dress. Papa put your trunk upstairs in your room."

Charlotte obediently trudged inside, but stopped in the kitchen to put her flower in a tin cup of water. She went upstairs to change into an old work dress.

She squealed in delight at her new bedroom. Papa had already put her old familiar furniture in place, but there was something new! A little yellow-polished oak desk stood just below the window. It had four small drawers and a lid that pulled down to reveal cubby holes of different sizes and a built-in box to hold pencils. Charlotte sat on the matching chair and admired the softly polished wood. She set the tin cup on top and raced across the hall to the boys' room. There was another desk there, like hers, but finished in a dark stain. She rushed down the stairs, two at a time. Mama was in the living room hanging curtains.

"Mama!" she exclaimed. "It's the most perfect little desk! Where did it come from?"

Mama looked down from the chair she stood on and smiled. "A special gift from your father! When Papa was visiting Mr. Cadieu before we arrived, he saw that Claire had a beautiful little desk. He thought that desks would be a nice surprise for you and the boys. Mr. Cadieu was able to order them from a local craftsman for Papa. Such an important man of Island Mine can get things done quickly it seems!

"But really, Charlotte, you must learn not to shout so. It isn't becoming to a lady to raise her voice. Now step up on that other chair and help me with these curtains. Will, the broom is in the pantry. You may sweep the floor, so we can put the rugs down."

Mama handled the curtains lovingly. They were real lace and had come with her from England. Mama's grandmother had crocheted them many years ago. Mama was proud of her fine linens and furniture and paintings that had once belonged to her ancestors.

"I do believe we could use a fire in that big fireplace tonight," said Mama. "The nights here will be cool, I think." She shivered and pulled her wool shawl close around her shoulders.

"There," she said, as they hung the last curtain. She looked around the cozy room with satisfaction. "Robin can hang the pictures, and with the rugs on the floor, this place will feel like home. Charlotte, the men brought crates of food down to the cellar. Will you please go down and put the canned goods on shelves for me?"

Charlotte lit the kerosene lamp and replaced its tall chimney. She held the light in front of her as she made her way down the dark cellar stairs. There were several crates piled on the dirt floor, their lids already pried loose. She opened one and found apples. Russets, she noted with delight. She selected one, wiped it hard on her white apron, and bit deeply into it. Juice ran down her chin and she flicked it off with the back of her hand. She placed the russets gently in a large barrel. It wouldn't do to bruise even one, for one bruised apple would cause the whole lot to rot. A crate of potatoes was next, then one of turnips and another of carrots. She lifted several heavy hams onto pegs on the wall and placed glass jars of peaches and applesauce on one long shelf.

Then Mama's voice called down, "That's enough for now, Charlotte. Bring up one of those balls of butter for dinner."

Charlotte took the cover off a wooden tub and placed a lump of yellow butter in a small dish.

The table was set and Charlotte could smell something wonderful coming from a large pot in the center of the table. When she lifted the lid, steam poured out. A large mass of pork and beans bubbled in rich brown sauce. Fresh brown bread was sliced thickly on the breadboard, and beside each plate was a sauce dish containing canned pears. A mincemeat pie was cut into six thick wedges.

William and Robin were at the table, snatching bits of crust from the pie. Mama carried in a huge platter of fried fish. Nothing had ever smelled as good as that fresh fish!

When Papa came through the front door, Charlotte ran to him.

"Thank you for my perfect little desk, Papa!" He hugged her tightly and stroked her soft brown hair.

"You're welcome, little daughter. You are a good girl and Mama and I want you to have nice things. Now let's eat! This fresh island air gives me quite an appetite!"

After prayer Mama passed the hot fish and Papa served large helpings of pork and beans.

"Such kindness to strangers I've never seen," said Mama. "Mrs. Cliff, the lady who runs the boarding house, brought over the food this afternoon. Said she had to cook for eighty men anyway, she might as well lay on a little extra for us. Such a generous soul! And I can only imagine all she has to do, cooking for a whole boarding house of miners! She likely knew that after our long day, we'd be eating cold meat with bread and butter."

Papa nodded. "She is a fine woman. Came over from Wisconsin three months ago. Her husband drowned in a fishing accident, I understand. You'll find these islanders very friendly and helpful, Elizabeth. With only 130 people here at Island Mine, we all have to look out for each other. Now let's hear what you've all been up to today." He bit into a slice of bread spread thickly with butter.

"I helped Mama!" chirped William. "I swept and dusted and carried in water and wood for a fire. Mama said we could have a fire in the fireplace tonight. Can we, Papa? And make some popcorn?" William licked mincemeat from his fingers and looked eagerly at Papa.

"That sounds fine, son! How about you, Rob? Did you find the mine all right?"

Robin nodded happily. "It isn't far. There are a couple boys a little older than me who are working there this summer too. Mr. Cadieu says I might come over tomorrow. I mean Monday," he corrected himself. The next day was Sunday. The mine was always closed on Sundays.

"How about you, Charli? How do you like your new friend?" Papa's eyes twinkled.

"Oh Papa," she began earnestly. "I've never met anyone like Claire. She isn't much older than me, but she knows everything about the forest! Her Gram taught her, she says. She knows about trees and flowers and birds and everything."

Papa said seriously, "Claire's Gram has quite a story to tell. She was raised in Canada and came over here with her husband in 1834. He worked for the American Fur Company on Isle Royale for several years. He drowned when his boat sank off Menagerie Island. Most women would have gone back home, but she stuck it out. Remarried a miner who came to the Smithwick Mine in 1840. He was killed in a mining accident after they had been married just six months. She raised Claire's mother on her own and survived by taking in boarders and laundry. She returned to Copper Harbor for awhile when the mines closed down, but was the first one to come back to Isle Royale when her son-in-law became the manager of the Island Mine Company. Life is a bit easier for her now. Not that you'd ever hear her complain, though." Papa finished his tea and pushed back his chair.

"Come Charlotte, let's get the dishes done quickly, and then we'll have our fire and popcorn," said Mama as she stacked dishes.

Jumbled thoughts chased each other through Charlotte's mind as she scrubbed the dishes in hot soapy water. She couldn't wait to meet Gram. But what happened to Claire's mama? Claire never spoke of her.

William's impatient voice brought her out of her thoughts. "Come on, Charli. You washed that plate three times. My feet are cold and the fire's warm in the parlor. Hurry up!"

She flicked a soap bubble and it landed on his nose. They laughed and dried the silverware quickly.

Papa sat in his large leather chair, smoking his pipe and reading a newspaper from Chicago. Mama rocked comfortably, crochet hook flashing in the firelight. Robin rattled the wire popcorn popper over the flames and William watched in fascination as the first kernels exploded into fluffy whiteness.

From her little footstool, Charlotte sighed, contented, and watched the flames lick at the birch logs in the fireplace.

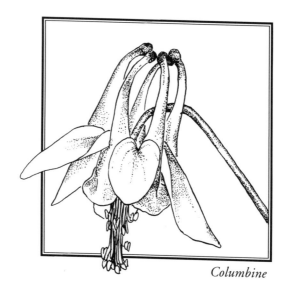

Columbine

CHAPTER 7

GRAM

WHEN CHARLOTTE AWOKE the next morning, she rubbed her eyes hard, trying to remember why she was in a strange room. Then she smiled to herself and snuggled cozily under the heavy quilts. She was on Isle Royale in her own pretty room, and it was Sunday. She reached out and lifted the tin cup holding the fragile orchid from the desk. She touched the lavender petals lightly, then set it down and sprang out of bed. She jumped when her bare feet hit the floor. It was cold. She hopped about from one foot to the other as she pulled on her best dress and buttoned up the back. Her fingers were stiff and clumsy as she smoothed the covers on the bed and pulled off her night cap. Carrying shoes in one hand and stockings in the other, she walked into the cozy kitchen.

Mama stood by the cook stove pouring puddles of pancake batter onto the hot iron griddle. Plump brown sausages sizzled and a large pot of oatmeal kept warm on the back of the stove.

"Good morning, daughter," Mama smiled pleasantly. "Put on a fresh apron and you may set the table. Papa is outside tending to the horses, and he will want breakfast when he comes in. We must hurry this morning. Sunday School starts at 9:00 a.m. and we don't want to be late the first day."

"Mama," Charlotte said suddenly as she placed the pitcher of cream on the table, "why do we have church in the school building? In Chicago, church was in its own building. What if the children at Sunday School don't like me? How will I behave and what will I say?" her lips trembled. Mama sat down beside her, drying her hands on her apron.

"Why, Charlotte," said Mama, "you've known the proper way to behave since you were a very little girl. Mind your manners and speak politely when spoken to. You will be fine, I'm sure. And to answer your first question, I suppose with so few people here at Island Mine there isn't a need for two buildings. Now be a brave girl and let's see a smile." Mama patted her cheek and smoothed a wrinkled hair ribbon.

Charlotte put on a brave face, but inside she felt full

of butterflies. She was always shy of meeting new people, and now she would have to meet all the children in town at once! She didn't enjoy her breakfast, and left her sugary donut untouched beside her plate.

It was a cool morning. The birds chattered noisily as Charlotte dragged her feet along the bumpy road. There were others hurrying, too, and Charlotte looked about anxiously for Claire's familiar face. A lady in a full bouncy skirt met them at the door.

"This must be Mrs. Avery!" she exclaimed in a booming voice. "And your lovely children! We've so been looking forward to meeting you.

"You may come with me, little girl. I'll show you to your class." Mrs. Jones took hold of Charlotte's hand and guided her toward a far corner of the large room. She looked back at Mama and Papa and they gave her an encouraging smile.

There were twelve other boys and girls in Charlotte's Sunday School class. She sighed with relief when Claire touched her arm lightly. They sat on a bench together, but didn't speak.

"Good morning children!" Mrs. Jones said in her booming voice. "We will begin with a few songs. Who has a favorite?"

They sang several songs and Charlotte knew all of them. Then Mrs. Jones told the story of Daniel and the Lion's Den. Charlotte had heard the story before, and she thought to herself that Papa could tell it much better than Mrs. Jones. But she tried to listen, because she knew that Mama would tell her it was important to be on her best behavior.

Later, Charlotte joined her family for the preaching service which was much like the ones Charlotte had attended at the large Methodist church in Chicago. After the service several men stopped to speak to Papa. She felt proud that he was an important man at Island Mine.

After Mama's good dinner of ham and beans, Charlotte sat on her little footstool by the fireplace and looked at Papa's big book of birds. The colorful pictures were pretty, but she wanted to play outside. Mama and Papa wouldn't allow boisterous activity on Sunday. She could only look at books, or quietly entertain William. When the evening meal was finished, Mama might let her go outside for a bit to get some fresh air.

At last the sun began to sink low in the west. Charlotte sat on the tree swing and gazed at the glorious colors of the sunset. The swing glided back and forth, and her feet just brushed the soft grass below. She began getting sleepy, but jerked wide awake when she heard footsteps crunching up the rocky drive.

Claire approached, holding the hand of the most unusual looking woman Charlotte had ever seen. She wasn't wearing a dress, but had on men's trousers held up by a pair of red suspenders. Her checkered flannel shirt was tucked into them. She had heavy boots on and a floppy brown hat that nearly covered her face. She carried a basket. Charlotte could smell something lovely from under the clean cloth on top.

"Charlotte Avery, I presume," said the lady, removing her hat to reveal hair as red as Claire's. Her face was deeply tanned and tiny lines were etched around her eyes and mouth. Her eyes were the palest blue, and Charlotte couldn't help staring.

"Go on and have a good look, child. I know you don't come across someone like me every day. My name is Marjorie Taylor and I'm Claire's grandma. She calls me Gram, so you might as well do the same. I baked these molasses cookies fresh this afternoon. Go on and help yourself."

Charlotte did help herself. Her eyes opened wide with delight when she took the first bite. Gram laughed happily. "Yep, you were right, Claire; she does like them just as much as you do. Have another, Charlotte."

Charlotte took another cookie. "Thank you, ma'am. I mean Gram. Would you like to come in?"

Gram nodded and stepped briskly through the open front door. "Claire has talked of nothing but the Averys since you two met yesterday. I thought I'd better come over and acquaint myself with Mrs. Avery."

Mama offered her hand and Gram shook it warmly. "Thank you so much for the cookies. The children will adore you. I haven't had a spare minute for baking yet," said Mama as she led Gram into the cozy parlor.

William couldn't take his eyes from the small lively woman. At last he spoke. "Are you a lady or a man? 'Cause you fix your hair like a lady, but I never saw a lady wear suspenders." He shoved a huge bite of cookie into his already full mouth. A spray of crumbs landed on Gram's sleeve.

Mama gasped in horror. "William! We don't speak to company that way! You apologize to Mrs. Taylor this instant." Mama's face was very red.

Gram laughed long and hard. "It's all right, Mrs. Avery. I have yet to meet a child who doesn't think I'm the most unnatural creature he ever laid eyes on. Come here, William, and sit on my lap. I know a few stories that you might find interesting."

Gram's stories were fascinating. She told of the days back in the 1830s when her husband, Thomas, worked for the American Fur Company on Isle Royale.

"Back then this island was called *Minong*," she said.

"And Indians were much more plentiful than white men. But there was never any trouble. We got on fine."

She told of the first era of mining on Isle Royale. "I expect you know all about it, Ian," she said to Papa. "A whole load of miners came over in the '40s. They had several camps, but after a few years people got discouraged with the fuss and bother of getting supplies on and off the island. Then the price of copper fell, so they all pulled out."

The evening passed quickly. Finally Mama looked at the tall mantel clock and gasped, "Mercy, it's way past bedtime for the children. Up you go now!" William had already fallen asleep, and Papa carried him upstairs. He put his sticky hands around Papa's neck and drowsily asked for one more cookie.

Charlotte lay wide awake in bed, thinking of Gram and earlier days on Isle Royale. "*Minong*," she said softly into the darkness. She liked how it sounded. After a few minutes she heard quiet voices downstairs and crept softly to the top of the stairs. Her eyes opened wide in surprise. Robin sat half-way down the stairs, a blanket draped around his shoulders. He beckoned to Charlotte and held one finger to his lips.

She crept toward him noiselessly. "What are you doing, Rob?" she whispered. "Why aren't you in bed?"

"Shhh," he whispered back. "For the same reason

you aren't, either. Gram is still here and I want to hear some more. You can stay only if you can keep perfectly still."

Charlotte solemnly promised. Robin pulled half of the blanket around her small shoulders. She tucked her chilled feet up under her long nightdress and snuggled close to him.

Gram spoke slowly in her low musical voice that was so like Claire's. Claire slept on a soft cushion by the fireplace.

"When I was at the other end of the island last week I pulled ashore and took a walk," said Papa. "I came across a gravestone marked, 'Charlie Mott, died on Isle Royale, 1845.' The stone was all by itself. Do you know anything about that, Gram?"

Gram set her teacup down on the dainty china saucer and looked at Papa with a steady gaze. "Indeed I do. Charlie Mott was married to Angelique. They were half-breeds—French and Indian. I knew Angelique quite well. She lived in Copper Harbor for awhile after leaving Isle Royale. She had a gruesome tale to tell about the death of Charlie, and I heard it straight from her lips." Mama and Papa leaned forward in interest as Gram began.

"There were mining interests on Isle Royale as early as 1840, as you know. One of the owners was a man named Mendenhall. He was a distrustful, suspicious fellow, and he feared that some evil would befall his mine and property if left alone during the winter of '45. So he convinced Charlie to come over for the winter and watch the place. Charlie needed the job, so he came over in the fall with Angelique. Mendenhall wanted them right away and did not give them much time to get supplies together. He promised to send a boat over with their winter provisions.

"Well, Charlie and Angelique waited and waited for those provisions to arrive. The small amount of food they had brought with them ran out in a few weeks time. The weather turned cold and finally the whole harbor froze over, but the supply boat had not come. There were no other people here, so they faced the long winter alone, with no supplies.

"They ate bark and moss and grew weaker and weaker from hunger as the weeks passed. Charlie was worse off than Angelique right from the start. She watched him wither away right before her eyes. Just about broke her heart to see him so thin, and at times quite out of his mind. She was bad off too, of course, but must have been made of tougher stuff. Charlie finally starved to death and Angelique put him in a little shed next to their cabin. She had no weapon and the thick ice made fishing impossible.

"Then one day, when the hunger was at its worst, she got an idea. She pulled a few strands of long hair from her head and fashioned them into a snare. She placed the snare outside in the snow and watched. At last, after about giving up hope, a rabbit came along and got caught in the snare. She was able to stay alive for the remainder of the winter in that way.

"In the spring the ice melted in the harbor. One day a boat pulled up to shore. Inside it were several men, one of them being Mendenhall. When Angelique told him about Charlie, he cried out, 'I sent a boat over with your supplies! I don't know why it never reached you.' Angelique was told later that he had never sent a boat at all. She got the men to bury Charlie decently and went home to her mother shortly after. She lived in Copper Harbor until just a few years ago, when I heard that she passed away."

Charlotte and Robin stared at each other, wide-eyed. Then they heard footsteps and jumped to their feet, slipping silently up the stairs and into bed. Charlotte lay there awake for some time, listening to the quiet night sounds outside her window. She thought of Angelique Mott all alone for a winter on Isle Royale. The down quilt was cozy, but Charlotte shivered before finally turning over and falling into a troubled sleep.

CHAPTER 8

PIERRE DUCHARM

THE NEXT FEW WEEKS were busy ones in the Avery home. As soon as the sun was up Papa went to work at the mine. He supervised the work crew as they built the wooden framework for the mine shafts. Charlotte liked the miners with their rough wool shirts, sturdy boots, and brown canvas hats. She liked their interesting and unfamiliar accents. They came to Island Mine from Ireland, England, Germany, and Scandinavia. Some of them barely spoke English, but worked hard and were well-liked in the village.

Robin's job at the mine was pumping the bellows. It was an important job, for he was responsible for supplying the men with fresh air as they worked underground. He loved working among the strong British and Europeans. He was proud of Papa and knew that all the men respected him.

Mama had much to do in the house, and most days she kept Charlotte inside to help until afternoon. Each day of the week had its own special duties. On Monday Charlotte helped Mama wash clothes in the big tin washtub. She disliked washing days. The wet laundry was heavy and she always got soaked lifting the wet things onto the clothesline. On Tuesday the clean clothes were sprinkled and ironed. Mama said that Charlotte was too young to handle the hot iron, so she played with William while Mama saw to the ironing.

Wednesday was cleaning day. Charlotte dragged the heavy rugs outside and beat them with a stick until no more dust flew out of them. William liked beating rugs too. He darted between them, hiding, when they hung on the line. He would shriek with laughter when Charlotte crept up behind him and grabbed him around the middle.

Thursday was sewing and mending day. Mama had taught Charlotte to knit and crochet when she was seven years old. She knitted thick woolen socks and mittens for the whole family.

Fridays were fun. Mama's baking filled the whole house with delicious smells. She gave Charlotte some dough and she made tiny loaves of bread to share with William. Once she made a whole little family of bread people.

The best day of all was Saturday. Then she was free to run and play outside, enjoying the fresh air. Most of the time she was with Claire. They had grand times together. Claire had been a frail child, prone to bouts of sickness. Gram spared her all but the lightest housework and she herself joined her granddaughter outdoors as much as possible.

Charlotte loved to explore the great island wilderness with Gram and Claire. Sometimes William went along with them, but his small legs soon grew tired and he would beg to be carried. So usually the Saturday outings were reserved for the happy trio of girls.

One Saturday late in June, Gram packed a picnic lunch and they set out through the woods. The day was mild, and the radiant sun turned Lake Superior into a sheet of glittering diamonds. It shone on the green-silver leaves of tall aspen and birch trees and transformed the deep forest into a magical fairy wonderland. Gulls swooped down low over the water, their beaks wide open and wailing. Black-and-white butterflies glided gently on the breeze, every now and then fluttering to a delicate landing on a colorful wildflower or tall blade of grass. Bees buzzed about busily, intent on their task of collecting pollen. Overhead the sky was deep blue. Thin wisps of clouds floated by, looking as if an artist had painstakingly drawn them with the finest paintbrush.

Charlotte skipped along behind Claire, who hurried to keep up with Gram's brisk pace. When Charlotte spied an especially pretty plant or flower she would stop and ask Gram about it. Gram always knew their names. She had lived most of her life in the wilderness and knew more about birds and animals and flowers than anyone Charlotte had ever met.

There were sprinklings here and there of the tiny delicate fairy slipper, or Calypso, that Claire had given Charlotte the day they first met. To herself, Charlotte called them "friendship flowers." Gram said that they were a kind of orchid. Sometimes they found other types of orchids. Claire squealed each time they spotted the pink or yellow lady's-slipper. Gram would not let them pick those; she said that their fragile, perfect beauty belonged only in the woods. In open sunny spots were the perky red-and-yellow columbine with their heart-shaped leaves, and in cool shady areas were little gaywings, with dainty purple petals so like a pair of wings.

This day Gram would not say where they were going, only that it was a surprise. In the distance they heard a white-throated sparrow cheerily singing, "Oh Sweet Canada-Canada-Canada!" The notes were rich and pure. A rustling of leaves over her head caused Charlotte to glance up. A saucy gray jay stared back at her and cocked its head to one side. The bird hopped to the end of a moss-covered branch and seemed to examine the little brown-haired girl closely.

Gram backtracked to where Charlotte and the large jay stood contemplating each other. She chuckled, "He's a right one. As curious of you as you are of him. He'll likely follow us clear to Hay Bay." Then she slapped her hand over her mouth, but too late. Charlotte and Claire had already caught her slip.

"We're going to see Mr. Ducharm, aren't we Gram?" shouted Claire in excitement. "I hoped that's where we were going!" She did a happy jig in the middle of the path. "Maybe he'll have some fresh lake trout and we can fry one up for our lunch!"

Gram smiled as she replied, "That's what I'd planned. I brought along some bread and butter with blueberry preserves and a fresh-baked custard pie. That should go nicely with trout. Mr. Ducharm is partial to my custard pie, if I do say so myself," she finished with a twinkle in her eyes.

"Who is Mr. Ducharm?" asked Charlotte, now caught up in Claire's enthusiasm. "I never heard Papa mention that name."

Gram explained, "He's one of the old-timers on Isle Royale, like me. Not many people ever see him since he doesn't live near the mine. But he likes it that way. Keeps to himself mostly—likes the privacy. He and I go back a long way. He fished with my Thomas back in the '30s. I've been meaning to see him for quite some time, but just haven't made it over. He'll be mighty glad to see Claire, here. She's one of his favorites. And I know he'll be pleased to make your acquaintance too, Miss Charlotte."

Charlotte was curious. "Doesn't he get lonely? How does he catch the fish? What does he do with the fish he catches?"

"Oh, he salts the fish so it will keep for quite a while. Then there's a boat that comes around every couple of weeks or so that picks up the fish and takes it to markets on the mainland. But we'll soon be there, Charlotte. Then Mr. Ducharm can tell you about how it's done."

A little while later, they came out of the woods into a clearing. The bay spread out before them in a shimmering blue mass. A stretch of land poked out into the bay like a long bony finger. Near the edge of the water stood a cabin built of logs. The chinks had been filled tightly with mud, and a stone chimney stood tall above the cedar-shingled roof. Beside it a dock reached into the bay and on the end of it was a crude shack. A long, low, white-painted boat, with its sail lowered, was pulled up on shore near a net reel. The ground all about was littered with wooden crates and tools. The smell of fish permeated the air.

"Halloo!" hollered Gram. Her loud voice broke the silence and startled a flock of gulls that hovered near the dock. They set up a terrible wailing racket. The door of the cabin opened with a creak, and a tall man with iron-gray hair and leathery-looking face stepped out. When he saw them his eyes lit up merrily.

"Well, would you look who's here! And just in time for lunch, too! I just stoked up the fire and was about to lay a big trout on the griddle. *Mon dieu*, it's good to see you, Margie, and why do you stay away so long?" He pecked her cheek and embraced Claire strongly.

"We brought along a new friend, Mr. Ducharm. This is Charlotte Avery. Her papa is the construction leader at Island Mine."

When Pierre Ducharm's gaze fell on Charlotte, he suddenly stepped back, tripped over a wooden crate and sat down hard. He held his hand to his chest, breathing rapidly and staring at Charlotte.

Gram rushed to him and took his large hands in her

small ones. "What is it Pierre? Is it your heart? Quickly, Claire, go fetch some cold water and a cloth…"

"No, no. I'm all right," he interrupted impatiently. "My heart is as strong as yours, Margie."

"Is it me, Mr. Ducharm? What did I do to upset you?" Charlotte blinked back tears.

"It's not your fault, child. You've done nothing wrong." He beckoned to her and gravely touched her long dark braids. "You just gave me a shock is all. I once had a little girl of my own. She looked a great deal like you. She drowned when she was ten years old."

Charlotte gasped, "I'm terribly sorry, sir. I could go if you like," her lips trembled and she looked anxiously from Claire to Gram.

Mr. Ducharm stood up and brushed off the seat of his canvas trousers. "No more talk like that now! You've walked a long way, and I'm delighted to see you, *all* of you," he added with emphasis. He took hold of Charlotte's and Claire's hands. "It's not every day a lonely old man gets three lovely callers. Now come on inside and let's have that fish. If my guess is right, Margie, you've got one of those custard pies that makes my mouth water in that hamper." His eyes sparkled at Gram.

She gave him a pleased smile and they entered the cabin.

"It was a long walk and I'm no spring chicken," said Gram. "But we won't stay long. I know you're busy at this time of year."

"Nonsense," he said, settling the question. "You'll stay for a good visit. Charlotte here might like to learn a thing or two about fishing."

The cabin had just one room which served as kitchen, bedroom, and living room. A bunk was shoved up against one wall, covered with a blue-and-white plaid blanket. Another wall held cupboards and the cook stove. A crude wooden table was pushed up against the wall beside the stove, and on the opposite side of the room, coats, trousers, hats, and mittens hung from pegs hammered into the thick logs.

A large fish lay on a plate next to the stove. A bit of grease sizzled and popped on the griddle as it heated. A glass canning jar filled with fragrant blue-and-yellow violets sat on the window sill. An old rocking chair and a small three-legged stool completed the furnishings. It was tiny, but snug and cozy, and neat as a pin. It smelled of pipe tobacco and wood shavings and fresh fish.

Charlotte had never seen a cleaner, more charming home and she told him so. He grinned, "*Oui*, it's good enough for me, all right. I don't need nothin' fancy. Just me and old Jacques here and he's so lame now he mostly just lies on the rug and watches the flies buzz by."

Claire gave the old collie a pat on his soft gray head and his tail thumped the floor in appreciation.

"Well now," said Pierre, "this fish will make us a fine lunch." He flipped it over and it sizzled loudly, sending out delicious waves of smell.

"You two will find plates and forks in that cupboard," he said, pointing. "The plates are a little chipped, but they'll have to do."

Claire buried her nose in the fragrant violets and breathed deeply. "Mmmm, so lovely. I haven't seen any violets around Island Mine."

Pierre looked embarrassed. "*Oui*," he said. "Some folks might think an old seadog like me wouldn't like flowers, but I need my bit of color. Kind of cheers up the place."

Lunch had never tasted so good. Pierre complimented Gram's custard pie so many times that she blushed with pleasure. "The secret is in the crust. Anyone can make a custard, but it takes a good bit of practice to turn out a proper pie crust."

While Gram cleared away the dishes, Claire and Charlotte sat with old Jacques on his rug and stroked his thick fur. Pierre lit his pipe and spoke from his rocking chair. "I have some nets to check this afternoon near Siskiwit Bay. How would you ladies like to come along? I could take you back to the big dock, save you a long walk home."

Claire leapt to her feet, her eyes shining. "Oh could we Gram? It would be such fun, and Charli has never been out in a fishing boat."

Gram considered, "It *would* save us that long walk back, but it would be way out of Pierre's way."

He rocked slowly. "It would be a pleasure. I don't often get over that way. I deserve a little vacation every now and then, don't I?"

So it was settled. "Margie," he said quietly, "you and Claire go out to the boat. Charlotte and I will be out shortly. Something I want to show her in my trunk."

Charlotte hadn't noticed the trunk before. It was old and brown, with leather hinges and rusty buckles. Pierre knelt down beside it and lifted the lid. It smelled strongly of cedar chips. He reached in and pulled out a small bundle wrapped in a yellowed linen cloth. Pierre's hands trembled as he unwrapped it carefully. Inside was a rag doll. She was perfectly made with soft cotton material. She had soft brown yarn hair and black shoe-button eyes. Her dress was flowered calico and on her feet she wore white silk stockings and tiny leather shoes.

Pierre's voice faltered when he held it out to Charlotte. "This belonged to my little Amy," he said with tears in his eyes. "Her mama made it for her before she was born. She surely loved this little doll. I'd like for you to have it. Dolls should have little girls to love them and play with them, not be stored away in an old box."

Charlotte sat on the floor beside Pierre and put her small arms around his broad shoulders. "I'm so sorry your little girl died, Mr. Pierre. She must have been a wonderful girl. I'll love the doll and think of your Amy whenever I look at her."

Pierre patted Charlotte's hand tenderly and brushed away his tears with a callused hand. "We'd best be going."

Lake Superior's blue water was beautifully calm as the boat glided smoothly into the bay. When they reached open water, wind filled out the large sail and Pierre laid down his oars. He showed the girls how to hold out crusts of bread for the gulls flying overhead. They squealed with excitement each time one of the white-and-gray sea birds swooped down and plucked the bread from their fingertips.

Charlotte was leaning over the edge of the boat

when a sudden eerie wail nearby nearly caused her to topple into the water. "A wolf!" she cried. "I thought I just heard a wolf!" She eyed the shoreline nervously.

Pierre laughed. "You just heard your first loon, little girl. Many people mistake their call for the howl of a wolf. There it is, over there!" He pointed at a large black-and-white bird near the shore.

Charlotte gasped; it was so beautiful! The head was black and a band of white encircled the long graceful neck. Its wings were black with white spots. It turned into the sunlight and Charlotte looked into its red eyes.

"Oh, how lovely," she breathed. "Wait until I tell Rob and Will about this."

It wasn't long before they reached the place where Pierre left his nets. When he heaved them into the boat, fish fell in a shining, shimmering cascade. Their fins caught the light and gleamed silvery.

With fish flopping on their feet and many cheerful thanks to Pierre, they soon stepped onto the dock in Siskiwit Bay. Claire's father was there with his wagon and he joined them.

"Well, it looks like someone had a fine day! And I caught you just in time to give you a ride home. Hop in, girls!"

Charlotte climbed wearily into the wagon. It had been a wonderfully exciting day and she was sleepy. Gram had to shake her to wake her up when they reached the Avery house.

She slipped inside, clutching her precious doll to her chest. "Oh, Mama, we had such fun," she whispered sleepily. "We rode in Mr. Pierre's fishing boat, and ate trout, and heard stories, and I heard a loon, and look what he gave me."

Mama led her upstairs and gently unbraided Charlotte's brown hair as she tumbled into bed, the rag doll tucked in firmly beside her.

Canada Dogwood

CHAPTER 9

Rock Harbor Lighthouse

THE COOL DAYS OF JUNE gave way to warmer ones of July, and July slowly melted into August. The long days grew warmer and the nights cooler. The winds increased on Lake Superior and some days the waves in the bay would be capped with white foam. The forest was changing. White blossoms of Canada dogwood gave way to Christmas-like bunches of red berry clusters. Where yellow flowers had once adorned the corn lilies, there were now dark blue berries. White doll's-eyes and red baneberries added to the riot of color carpeting the forest floor.

The summer had been dreamlike for Charlotte, frolicking outdoors in the pure island air until her skin tanned a dark brown. Papa would playfully pull her long braids and call her his little Indian.

On the fifth day of August, Charlotte stood beside

the cook stove, a spatula in one hand and a pitcher of pancake batter in the other. She carefully tipped the pitcher and poured four puddles onto the hot griddle. She watched carefully for the tiny bubbles that would start to form.

"Don't let them get too brown, Charlotte," Mama called from the pantry where she was rolling biscuit dough.

"I know, Mama," said Charlotte, as she carefully turned the round pancake. It was golden brown and crispy around the edges.

"These are the best ones I've made yet," she thought to herself proudly. Mama had been teaching her for the past few days and the family had dutifully eaten all of her scorched attempts.

Robin came into the kitchen and crept up softly behind her, snatching at her apron strings. "Oh no, Charli's cooking again," he said with a groan, holding his stomach and pretending to be in pain.

Charlotte flicked a bit of batter at him. "You stop it, Rob. Mama says I'm doing better. Anyway, William likes my cooking, don't you, Will?"

William nodded eagerly and sidled up next to Charlotte defensively. "You do everything good, Charli. Rob's just jealous because he can't cook."

"Thank you, little brother," she said. "Are you ready

to make your pancake man?"

He stood on a chair beside the stove and put his small hand over Charlotte's. Together they poured batter to form the head, body, and two wee arms and legs.

At the breakfast table, Papa poured thick dark maple syrup over his pancakes and looked at Charlotte. "The day after tomorrow is your birthday, daughter. How would you like to spend it?"

Charlotte stopped cutting her piece of ham, startled. "I completely forgot! I've *never* forgotten my birthday before!" Mama and Papa always let the children plan a special day on their birthdays, and turned it into a holiday for the whole family.

"It just so happens," said Papa, "that Mr. Cadieu has offered to take several families sailing out to Rock Harbor Lighthouse for the afternoon. If you like, you could ask Claire to join us, and you girls could fix us a picnic lunch to take along. How does that sound for an eleventh birthday, Charli?"

Charlotte's eyes glittered. "That would be perfect, Papa! And I know that Claire will want to come along. Can we make some fried chicken to take, Mama? And I could make the cake. I know how!" She was too excited to finish her breakfast. "May I go ask Claire right now?"

Mama laughed. "You might as well go. Don't stay

long though. I need your help inside today."

Charlotte kissed Mama's cheek and wrapped her arms around Papa's neck. His beard tickled her nose. "Thank you, Papa," she whispered and then shot out the door, letting it slam behind her.

Claire was excited about the birthday trip. "Oh, won't it be glorious fun, Charli? I've never been to the lighthouse—Father has though." They chatted happily for a few minutes, making plans for the big day. Even helping with laundry did not seem so bad with a birthday picnic to look forward to.

The next day Mama fried a great basket full of chicken. Charlotte boiled a dozen eggs to eat with salt. She beat cake batter vigorously with a wooden spoon. There would also be tiny pickles and bread and butter with raspberry preserves.

The cake turned out nicely and when Charlotte finished decorating it with white sugar frosting, she thought it was perfect.

The morning of her birthday dawned cloudy and gray. A few drops of rain pattered on the windows lightly. But then the sun broke through the clouds and shone brightly.

"Happy birthday, Charli!" yelled William, as she came down the stairs. "I made this for you. Well, Papa helped too, and Rob."

Charlotte gasped. She had never seen such a pretty picture.

"It's your favorite wildflower, Charli, the one Gram calls fairy slipper and you call 'friendship flower.'"

"It's perfectly lovely, Will," she exclaimed. "How did you make it?"

"Well," he explained importantly, "we picked the flowers and put them between the pages of one of Papa's heavy books, to dry out and get flat. That took a long time. I peeked once in awhile to see if they were flat yet. Then we put them on the cardboard and pasted them down. Papa and Rob made the frame and Mama found a piece of glass to fit. Do you really like it, Charli?"

"It's the best present I ever had," she answered, hugging him tightly. "I'll hang it right by my bed so it will be the first thing I see when I wake up every morning."

"Come children," called Mama. "We must eat and be on our way. Claire is here, Charlotte."

Claire held out her gift. It was a pretty piece of coral that Charlotte had often admired. She gave her friend a hug.

"I think I'm the luckiest girl in the world to have such wonderful friends and family."

The storm during the night had stirred up Lake Superior, and waves crashed angrily against the dock. Mama was pale with seasickness before the boat had even left Siskiwit Bay. Papa sat beside her stroking her hair.

"I'll be fine once we get there," she said weakly. "These waves always get the best of me. I'm sorry, Ian."

Papa kissed her forehead gently. "I know you can't help it, my dear. The ride won't be too long this time."

There were several other families on the boat. William stayed close to Charlotte and Claire. The rolling sea scared him, but he couldn't be persuaded to leave his sister. He clung tightly to her hand as she leaned over the rail, peering into the churning water below. Charlotte wasn't a bit seasick. She loved days like this, when mighty Lake Superior, queen of the Great Lakes, chose to remind those who traveled on her that she was the largest, angriest body of fresh water in the whole country.

Gulls wailed into the wind as they bobbed up and down on the waves. On the journey Mr. Cadieu's first mate pointed out interesting things to Charlotte and Claire. He was a young man, barely twenty-one, but he had traveled on Lake Superior since he was fourteen. He had white-blond hair and a mischievous smile. He knew a great deal about Isle Royale and her surrounding waters. His name was Sandy. Charlotte liked him at once.

His hair blew every which way in the wind. "That's Menagerie Island ahead," he yelled, pointing. "Sometime in the next few years there is to be a lighthouse there. It'll be a great help to us who travel a lot around Siskiwit Bay. Right now Isle Royale has only one light, the one at Rock Harbor."

Charlotte gazed at long, narrow Menagerie Island and tried to imagine a lighthouse there, all surrounded by wild and lonely Lake Superior. They sailed close to shore and Sandy pointed out Chippewa Harbor, Saginaw Point, and Conglomerate Bay. There were many small islands and some of the names sounded funny. There was Caribou Island and Outer Hill Island and Shaw Island.

In the distance a white object gleamed in the bright sunshine. Charlotte pointed, "Is that Rock Harbor Lighthouse, Sandy?"

He nodded. "That's it, all right. It was built in 1855, so she's almost twenty years old now. The light has been extinguished since 1859 because the miners of the '40s left the area, and it wasn't thought necessary any longer. But with the renewed mining activity, the light will likely be relit sometime soon." He excused himself to prepare the boat for docking.

"Father says that nobody lives here now," said Claire. "But he brought the keys along so we can look inside. I wish Gram had come, but she said she wanted to get some baking done. I think Pierre Ducharm was coming for a visit," she added naughtily.

The lighthouse was in full view. It looked different from the one in Copper Harbor. The tower was tall and white, and attached to it was the low keeper's quarters. The windows were covered with iron bars. Tall evergreens surrounded it on three sides, leaving the front open to the lake.

On the dock, Mama plucked at Charlotte's dishevelled braids and laughed. "You are a sight, child. The wind has pulled your braids apart. You may as well keep your hair down until we get home. Let's find a nice place on the beach to have our picnic."

Charlotte and Claire raced ahead to the rocky shore. Waves pounded the rocks. Charlotte stripped off her stockings and shoes and dipped her toes cautiously in the water. She winced, but continued wading until the waves lapped at the hem of her dress. Her feet and ankles were numb, and she went quickly back to shore.

"Too chilly for a swim, eh?" laughed Claire's father.

"That's Lake Superior for you—even in the warmest months of the summer the water temperature might never rise above 40 degrees."

Shoes back on, the girls raced up a rocky ledge. When they reached the top they called down happily, "Up here! Let's have lunch up here—you can see everything!"

Papa, Mama, and Mr. Cadieu laughed. "It's her birthday. I guess she can have her way." They trundled up the hill more slowly. Claire's father led the way, while Papa carried the heavy wicker hamper behind Mama, who held up her skirts as she climbed.

The fried chicken was delicious. Charlotte beamed with pride when even Robin complimented her cake. After lunch they sat quietly on the warm rocks, admiring the panorama stretched out before them. They could see other small islands with their orange-covered rocks and tall trees towering into the blue sky. Far away across the lake, the sky seemed to melt into the blue-green water.

They scooted down the hill. Claire's father jangled keys in one hand. He leaned on the door to the lighthouse with all his weight, but it wouldn't budge. Papa leaned heavily against it too, and finally it opened with a rusty creak. The interior was dark. A few pieces of furniture cluttered the small living space. A family of mice had made a soft nest in the cushion of a red velvet chair. The white paint on the stone walls was cracked and peeling.

The entrance to the tower revealed a long, narrow flight of stairs. Charlotte touched the stone wall. It was cool and damp. She drew her hand back quickly. They clumped up the iron stairs, sending bits of dirt sifting down below. At the top of the tower was the large lens of glass set in brass. Claire's father told them about the life of a lighthouse keeper.

"It's a lonely life for these fellows. They come out early in the spring and stay until a boat comes for them late in the fall. Their main job is to keep the glass on the light clean and the outside windows free of ice." He led them outside to an iron platform that circled the top of the tower. "The keeper has to come out here in bad weather and clear all the ice off the windows. The passing ships must be able to see the light at all times."

Charlotte held onto the cold iron railing and looked down. She felt dizzy being so high up and quickly thumped back down the stairs.

"I like it much better on the ground!" said Charlotte in relief. "I guess I'll never be a lighthouse keeper. I wouldn't want to hang over the edge up there every day!" She shivered.

They joined the other children on the beach, who crouched down, examining pretty rocks and interesting pieces of driftwood. Charlotte picked up several shiny rocks and put them carefully in her pocket. She found a piece of driftwood shaped like a duck, and kept that too.

After awhile some of the children began playing games. Charlotte joined in; she was shy at first, but was soon yelling with the others. They played leap frog and crack the whip and king of the hill. She had never had such fun. She screamed and laughed, her cheeks flushed and hair blowing loose and free in the wind.

At last the sun began to sink low in the west. They climbed on board the boat and waved good-bye to the silent, lonely lighthouse.

Charlotte was sleepy. She laid her head on Papa's shoulder. As she drifted off to sleep, the waves rocked the boat like a giant cradle. She didn't wake up until they entered Siskiwit Bay.

"Papa," she said dreamily, "this was the best birthday ever." Papa smiled and planted a gentle kiss on her forehead.

"It was a fine day, little daughter. I'm glad we could all come and enjoy it together."

CHAPTER 10

VISITING THE MINE

"MAMA," asked Charlotte as she pulled the broom across the kitchen floor, "why do I have to go to school? Why can't I stay home and help you? I would work real hard, I promise!" She looked earnestly at Mama. Mama set aside the quilt block she was sewing.

"We've been through all this before, Charlotte. You've always gone to school, and you will go here as well. I don't know what makes you so nervous. It isn't as if you'll be alone, you know. Robin and William will be there, and you'll have Claire."

William looked at Charlotte eagerly, laying down his picture books. "Yes, Charli! I'm going with you this year! I can't wait for recess!"

Charlotte rumpled his gold curls and tilted his chin up. "You have jelly on your face, little brother." She wiped the corners of his mouth with her handkerchief.

Papa sat quietly reading in his big chair by the fireplace. After a few minutes he put the heavy book aside.

"You know," he began, "it's high time you children had a proper look at the mine. Rob here sees it every day, but Charli and Will have never spent much time there. School starts next week and then there won't be time to go. What say you two tag along with me tomorrow and see what your papa does all day?" His eyes twinkled as he looked from Charlotte to William.

"Hooray, hooray," yelled William, dumping a lapful of wooden blocks on the wool rug as he jumped up. He grabbed Charlotte's hands and she whirled him about the room. She laughed because he was laughing. She had begged Papa for weeks to take her to the mine site.

The September morning was clear and sunny, but chilly. Charlotte pulled her shawl snugly around her shoulders and walked behind Papa. He carried William on his shoulders. Robin hurried ahead of them lugging the big tin dinner pail.

The miners had already arrived at work when they got there. Charlotte thought they looked much more comfortable in their rough work clothes than in their Sunday shirts and somber black suits.

Several deep shafts had been sunk into the rock. Heavy timbers lined them, running crosswise and lengthwise down the shaft. Charlotte peered down into one deep hole and then said to Papa, "How do they know where the copper is? Do they just start digging anywhere and hope that they get lucky now and then?"

"That's a good question, Charli. Some of the men go out in a boat and look at the rocks from a distance. Sometimes they can see veins of copper running through the rock. Sometimes the vegetation is burned off so the veins can be more easily seen."

Charlotte thought that she would like the job of riding around in a boat on Lake Superior hunting for coppery-colored rocks.

Papa continued. "If a vein looks promising, a shaft is sunk and blasted out. Many men who work at the mine spend all their time above ground. They cut timber, erect machinery, clear land, and remove waste rock. They're called surface men and wear leather boots, canvas trousers, red flannel shirts, and low-crowned, broad-rimmed hats. They're paid one dollar a day."

Papa led them to a small log building. Inside was a hot fire and many types of tools. This was where the blacksmith worked. His job was to sharpen drills, repair metal work, and make shoes for the great work horses. The blacksmith was a large man with a big booming voice. His shirt was rolled up to the elbows and the muscles stood out like bars of iron. He bent down and peered into William's staring eyes.

"Would you like to see how a horseshoe is made, young man?" he bellowed.

William ducked behind Papa and peeped out nodding his head.

"Fine!" boomed the great burly man. "Stand in the doorway and don't get too close to the fire!" He threw another log into the blazing fire and picked up a piece of iron. He held it in the fire with a long-handled clamp until it glowed red from the heat. Then he quickly clanged the red-hot iron down on an anvil and smacked it with a heavy hammer. Sparks shot out and scattered on the dirt floor. When the metal cooled too much to bend, he placed it back into the fire to reheat. He continued the process until the iron bent to the desired shape. Holding it in the long-handled clamp, he let it cool in a bucket of water. He tossed it to the ground and it landed at William's feet.

"Take it home with you, young fellow! And remember, a man who hangs a horseshoe over his door is a lucky man indeed!"

William picked up the new horseshoe, his eyes round. "Want to feel it, Charli? It's still warm! Papa, when I grow up I'm going to be a big strong black-smith like him!" He rolled up his sleeves and examined his small arms for traces of the muscles to come.

"What's that building, Papa?" asked Charlotte, laughing at William's capers.

"This is the cooper's shop," said Papa. "He has a very important job. He makes all the buckets that we use here. They must be made to hold a great deal of weight." There were buckets of all types and sizes inside—large ones, small ones, some with handles, and some without.

William picked up one and put it on his head, upside down. "Look at me! I'm a bucket-head! Hey, it's dark in here!"

Papa and Charlotte laughed. She lifted the bucket off his head. "You silly goose."

Papa guided them toward a shaft where men were working underground.

"Miners work very hard," said Papa. "They are paid per fathom dug. A fathom is six feet, so they are paid twenty dollars per six feet. They bring the ore up and it is shipped on Lake Superior to Sault Sainte Marie."

One of the miners paused to talk to Papa. "How far down in the ground do the shafts go?" Charlotte asked.

"An average of sixty feet," the miner answered

politely. "We climb down that ladder there and work eight to ten hours every day except Sunday. The ore is removed after we loosen it by blasting. We load ore into buckets at the bottom and they're pulled up with a hand-windlass or a horse-powered hoist."

He removed his hat and showed it to Charlotte and William. A candle was held to its front with a lump of clay. "Our candles are very important to us down there. It's pitch black without them." Charlotte felt the lump of clay and peered into the darkness of the shaft again. She was glad that she was outside in the bright sunshine.

The miner continued, "The main problems down there are water and ventilation. Your brother's job is very important to our operation. The bellows boy pumps air down the shaft so we always have oxygen to breathe." He tipped his hat to Papa and trundled down the steep ladder. Charlotte watched his descent until the flame from his candle was just a speck, and then disappeared completely.

They went to Papa's workshop. It was filled with tools and equipment. It smelled of new lumber, sawdust, and pipe tobacco. Then they went to eat lunch beneath a tall birch tree. Charlotte loved these tall skinny trees with their white bark. When the wind stirred the small leaves at the top, it made a wonderful rustling sound all its own.

For the rest of the afternoon William played in the clearing, searching for bits of copper ore to take home. Charlotte leaned against a tree and gazed at the wispy clouds in the sky. She thought of the miners with their work-roughened hands and slow smiles. She thought of them leaving home to go to a far-away country full of strangers... of working hard all day with no family to go home to at night. And in her mind she saw once again the small light from the miner's candle disappearing into the black hole.

Charlotte shivered and wrapped her shawl snugly around her shoulders. It frightened her to think of the dangers the miners faced every day, but without them there would be no Island Mine.

Papa's voice interrupted her thoughts. "Ready to go! Will, you're a sight! Mama will have you in the tub as quick as a wink!"

With a sigh Charlotte dusted off her skirt and ran to catch up with Papa and William.

CHAPTER 11

SCHOOL

THERE WAS A SMALL OVAL MIRROR that hung above Charlotte's wash basin. She carefully combed and braided her long thick hair and gazed at her reflection. It was the first day of school and Mama said that she might wear her Sunday hair ribbons. She stroked the scraps of rose-colored velvet with the tip of her finger and looked back in the mirror, dissatisfied with her reflection. She wished for red hair like Claire's, or curly gold hair like William's. But hers was dark brown and very straight. Mama used to try to curl her fringe of bangs, but the thick hair refused to bend. Mama would throw up her hands in exasperation.

When examined closely, her blue eyes contained tiny specks of green and brown. Her nose and ears were small. Too small, she thought to herself. Her full lips curved over white teeth. They were nice teeth, even and straight. Papa said that someday the boys would come running when she flashed her brilliant smile. She shivered in disgust at that thought. Boys could wait.

"Mercy, child, are you sick?" called Mama from the kitchen. "You'll be late for your first day of school if you don't finish up and eat your breakfast. Will and Rob are waiting for you!" Her voice trailed off and was replaced with the clatter of dishes.

She was too nervous to eat much breakfast. Mama let her go with a few gulps of milk and a piece of buttered toast in each hand.

"Off you go now!" Mama followed them to the end of the drive and gave each of them a peck on the cheek.

"Aw Mama!" Robin cried, embarrassed. He glanced around, fervently hoping that none of the older boys had seen.

"I'll have a hot lunch waiting for you at noon. Rob, straighten your collar, and Charlotte, you look after Will. And for goodness sake, cheer up!" She smiled after them encouragingly, wiped her hands on her apron, and walked slowly back to the house.

At the schoolyard, children of all ages ran about, running and skipping, tossing balls and jumping rope.

When the teacher appeared, ringing a small handbell, they rushed in and scurried into seats.

Miss McKinney was lovely, thought Charlotte, and she smelled nice too. She was tall and slender with fiery red hair pulled back into a loose bun. Tiny ringlets framed her kind face. Her pink cheeks were peppered with tiny freckles. Charlotte fell in love with her voice at once. It was deep and rich and full of laughter. Her accent was similar to Mama and Papa's, but more musical.

She told them about herself. "I was born in Ireland and have lived there all my life. This past spring I received a letter from my brother, Paddy, who works here at Island Mine. He told me that the school here was in need of a teacher, and would I like to come? Well, being always on the lookout for a great adventure, I promptly packed my bags and boarded the next ship for America. And here I am!" She smiled cheerfully.

"Now that you know a bit about me, I would like to get to know all of you. When it's your turn, please give me your name, where you came from, and what you most like to do in your free time. There are twenty-five of you in all—what a nice size for our school! After we finish, we'll play a game."

The children looked at each other in amazement.

Games in school! No one ever heard of such a thing. Each child took his or her turn. They had come to Isle Royale from England, Ireland, Germany, Finland, and Norway. Some of them had been born in America but still had some of the accent of their parents. Some, like Miss McKinney, had been in America only a very short time.

Samantha Jones said that she liked riding horses. Frank Mueller liked going fishing with his papa. Molly Swensen liked playing with her dolls. Claire's favorite activity was making molasses cookies with Gram. Then it was Charlotte's turn.

"A great thunderstorm on Lake Superior is my favorite thing," she said quietly. "I like to sit on the dock and watch the dark, angry clouds and the white jags of lightening and hear the thunder crash. Sometimes when it's especially loud it feels like it rumbles right through my insides. And I love the huge waves with their white caps when they crash against the rocks on shore."

Miss McKinney clapped her hands for attention. "Since we are all relatively new to this island, perhaps we can learn about it together. I am a firm believer that lessons we learn from nature are equally as important as those we get from books. Who can tell me some facts about Isle Royale?"

Hands shot up eagerly. "Isle Royale is about nine miles wide and forty-five miles long."

"Indians were here long before white men. They called the island *Minong*. That means 'a good place to be.'"

"Father says that the whole length of the island is a series of ridges and valleys. If there were a path that went from one end to the other, you'd be going up and down the whole way."

"There are many types of animals, but not as many as on the mainland, because they all have to either swim over or cross on the ice."

"My goodness!" exclaimed Miss McKinney. "Maybe I shouldn't be the teacher here at all! You all know so much! Can anyone tell me how this island came to belong to the United States?"

Robin raised his hand eagerly. "The captain of the *Precarious* told me about it. In 1783 when the Treaty of Paris was signed, Benjamin Franklin insisted that the boundary between the United States and Canada be drawn north of Isle Royale."

"Very good, Robin!" she exclaimed. "And although Isle Royale is much closer to Minnesota, Michigan was given control of the island in 1837, when Michigan became the first Lake Superior territory to be admitted to the Union. Now let's have our game!"

Five players were picked and went out of the room. These five arranged themselves in any order. Then they came running back in the room, ran around it once, and left again. The first one of those remaining in the classroom who named all the incoming ones in correct order got to pick five other players and it all started again.

The game was lively and soon they were all laughing and clapping. They quickly learned each other's names. When the game was over they fell into their seats, laughing and panting for breath.

Charlotte, William, and Robin had much to tell Mama when they went home for lunch.

"Oh Mama, Miss McKinney is just beautiful," said Charlotte. "She has the reddest hair, like Claire's. She has the loveliest dress and the sweetest smile. And guess what? She came from Ireland! That's near England where we came from! Her accent is kind of like yours and Papa's, only different. And guess what else..."

William clamped his hand over Charlotte's mouth. "Let me tell, Charli! We played a game! It was lots of fun and I got to run in school! I like school!"

Mama smiled as she dished up hot stew and cut thick slices of bread. "Likely it won't be all fun and games, son. What about you, Rob? You're awfully quiet."

"Aw, it's all right, I guess. I'd rather be at the mine with Papa, though, or out in the *Precarious* with Captain Petersen."

"Mama," said Charlotte, swallowing a mouthful of bread and jam, "Belinda James wasn't in school today. I wonder why not?" Belinda lived next door to Claire. Her father was the physician at Island Mine.

Mama sighed and sat down wearily. "That was bad news indeed. I heard just this morning that Dr. James and his family left the island. They didn't even pack up their furniture. Apparently Mrs. James had had enough of Isle Royale and being so isolated. She said that if he wouldn't take them back to Boston she would leave him and take Belinda with her. So he gave in and they left last evening. What this village will do all winter without a doctor I just don't know." Her worried hands made tiny creases in the white table-cloth.

"But we mustn't worry," she said briskly. "I have faith that God will take care of us; He always has before. Now scoot on back to school, you three! It's nice to see that smile again, Charli. I told you every-thing would be all right."

Mama was right. Miss McKinney knew some fun games, but she was also one for good hard work. In the afternoon she sorted them into classes and passed out books. There were four others in Charlotte's class: Claire, Sara Adams, Peter Barber, and Meghann O'Leary. Charlotte knew them well and was pleased that they would all be studying together.

"Children," said Miss McKinney to Charlotte's class, "you are going to do some writing for me today. Your assignment is to think about the last year and write one event that took place which really stands out in your mind. Make it as short or as long as you wish, but make it meaningful. Tell me how you felt; were you sad, happy, nervous, excited? Did your hands shake and your palms sweat? Would you do it again given the chance? If you have problems I'm here to help. But the idea should start with you." She flashed an encouraging smile and moved on to another class.

Charlotte stared at her empty slate for a long time and then began to write.

The Great Fire

Chicago is a large city in the state of Illinois. Its population is about 300,000. Papa says that the city is a giant melting pot, with people coming together from all over the world. I liked it there. There were many shops and schools and churches. Everything was made of wood—buildings, sidewalks, and even some streets.

Last summer we waited and waited for rain, but it never came. Chicago got drier and drier and finally one day a fire started. Once it started it didn't ever want to stop. It burned through the whole city. It jumped the river and chased people from their homes. Many of them ran for the protection of Lake Michigan. I was one of those people. I stood in the cold water and watched Chicago burn. I cried because I was scared and couldn't find my family. I cried because I thought they were burning up in the fire. But mostly I cried because everyone else that I could see was crying. I broke my leg that day, too, but that didn't hurt nearly so much as seeing all those people crying. My family started a new life when we left Chicago and came to Isle Royale. But sometimes I still think about all those tears that fell into Lake Michigan that day.

Bluebells

CHAPTER 12

VISITORS FROM ENGLAND

CHARLOTTE ENJOYED SCHOOL more with every day that passed. She and Sara and Meghann and Claire all became good friends. They played together at recess and strolled home together in the afternoons. Sara's father ran the general store. Mr. Adams was a jolly man—short and round and nearly bald. He wore tiny steel-rimmed spectacles and had a great booming laugh.

On an afternoon late in September Charlotte ran breathlessly into the store. Mama needed yeast for baking. Mr. Adams greeted her with his customary friendly smile. "Hello, little Miss Avery! What can I do for you today?" He reached behind the counter and handed her a stick of peppermint candy.

"Mama needs some yeast," she said, handing him a coin. While he wrapped the package she wandered about the store. There were shelves full of bolts of cloth: flannel and silk, muslin and cotton. She fingered a lovely pale pink silk and longed for the day when she would be grown up enough to wear the elegant fabric. There were barrels of pickles and crackers and cans of vegetables and great bins of flour and sugar. Long-handled tools leaned against the walls: shovels and picks and spades and axes.

"Here you go, Charlotte," said Mr. Adams, handing her the small bundle. "Tell your ma that I just got in some new fabric she might want to see and… oh my land, I nearly forgot! The *Precarious* came in this morning and there was mail on board. There's a letter for your ma. Came a long way too, from the looks of the stamp."

Charlotte peered closely at the strange stamp. "This is from England!" she cried. "Oh, Mama will be so excited! I must get home at once!"

"Mercy on us, child!" said Mama, when Charlotte burst through the front door. "Are you sick?" She put a cool hand on Charlotte's flushed cheek.

"No, Mama, nothing like that. Look, a letter! It's from England, isn't it? Who is it from?"

Mama looked closely at the small, neat handwriting. Then she quickly removed a hair pin and tore the letter open eagerly.

"It's from my brother Kent in London." She scanned the pages quickly, then sat down heavily, her dark eyes shining. "Kent and his family are coming to America! They will live in Boston, but are coming first to Isle Royale for a visit. They will arrive on September 25 and stay for three weeks."

She stopped reading and looked up. "September 25! That's tomorrow!" She looked at the date on the letter. "This letter was written in June!" She jumped to her feet and nearly knocked a vase of asters and daisies off the table.

"However will we be ready in time? There are a million things to do! Kent and his wife adopted a boy several years ago. Why, I think he's about your age, Charli! Oh, it's been so long!" Tears gathered in her eyes. "I've missed Kent so," she added softly.

Then she sprang into action. "Charli, run and tell Papa the news and take Will with you." She hurried into the pantry, mumbling to herself about pies and preserves and fresh fish.

The rest of the day was a frenzy of activity. Mama put everyone to work at a feverish pace. Robin carried in extra firewood. Papa made a bed in his office for Uncle Kent and Aunt Catherine. Cousin Chris would share Robin and William's room.

It was past midnight when they tumbled exhausted into bed. Charlotte's knees hurt from scrubbing the kitchen floor. "They better notice how clean it is," she grumbled to herself before she drifted off to sleep.

It seemed that she had no more than closed her eyes than William was tugging the covers from her shoulders. She yanked them back with a scowl. "It's cold, Will, go away and let me sleep!"

He tugged at the quilt again and jumped on the bed. "Mama says you have to get up, Charli! Papa is already hitching up the team to go down to the dock." He kissed her cheek and left a smudge of raspberry jam. Charlotte grabbed him around the middle and tickled him. He shrieked with laughter and they dashed down the chilly stairway.

The air outside was crisp and cool. A thin mist of fog was in the air. Charlotte buried her hands deep in her coat pockets as the horses trotted briskly down the bumpy road.

"Good thing Kent didn't wait any longer to come across," said Papa, shouting to be heard over the rumble of the wagon wheels. "Lake Superior won't be fit to travel on in another month or two," he added, eyeing the rolling waves.

"Likely they've had time to adjust to rough water,"

said Mama, her hands folded neatly in her lap. "They've just come off a ship on the Atlantic Ocean. I remember that trip like it was yesterday," she said with a shudder. Their voyage from England had been seven years before, but the memory had not faded with time.

Aunt Catherine and Uncle Kent stood on the deck of the large ship as it pulled up to the dock.

"He looks like Mama!" thought Charlotte, when she saw Uncle Kent's dark wavy hair, fair skin, and high cheek-bones. Aunt Catherine was nearly as tall as her husband, but fair-haired and freckled. They stepped onto the dock, cousin Chris resting his hand lightly on his mother's arm. They were greeted with eager hugs and kisses. When Charlotte came to kiss Chris' cheek, she stopped short in surprise. His clear green eyes stared past her, unseeing.

"You must be cousin Charlotte," he said warmly. "I've been so looking forward to meeting all of you."

"These are my brothers, Robin and William," she said shyly. The boys exchanged awkward handshakes and Robin looked embarrassed. Then Papa loaded their heavy trunk into the wagon and tied it securely with a length of stout rope.

Mama and Uncle Kent talked nonstop on the front wagon seat, with Aunt Catherine adding a comment or question now and then.

The children sat silent in the back. "Blind!" thought Charlotte. She had once seen a blind man in Chicago. She stared hard at Chris. "He has a kind face," she thought. "His eyes are a lovely shade of green," so much like the great lake she dearly loved. "Maybe he won't be so bad, for a boy."

William could control his curiosity no longer. "How come you can't see? And if you really can't see, why are your eyes open?"

Charlotte clamped a hand fiercely over his mouth. "That isn't polite, Will," she whispered harshly. "You mustn't ever talk like that!" Her face flushed scarlet and Robin pretended not to have heard.

But Chris laughed softly. "It's all right, Charlotte. Will has probably never seen a blind person before. Come, sit by me, little cousin."

The relatives fell in love with Isle Royale. Uncle Kent spent his days at the mine with Papa and took Aunt Catherine for long walks in the evening. Aunt Catherine insisted that she just be called "Cat." She helped Mama with the housework and asked endless questions about America. Together they pored over the latest books and papers that she brought from London. One evening Aunt Cat opened her trunk and brought out several bundles of various sizes, all wrapped in brown paper. She passed them out and everyone exclaimed in delight as each package was opened.

Papa's bundle contained a large stack of newspapers. Mama had a pair of white silk gloves. Robin received a real navigational compass. He was so overcome with awe that he forgot to say thank you. William squealed when he discovered his wooden soldiers with hand-painted uniforms and arms and legs that really moved. Charlotte loved her gift. It was a small heart-shaped locket hung on a gold chain.

Charlotte and Chris became fast friends. Chris was quiet and gentle. He loved to be outdoors in the warm sunshine and cold wind. Charlotte would rush home from school and lead him into the forest. He held onto her arm lightly. She never ceased to be amazed that he never tripped over roots and rocks that always seemed to cause her, a sighted person, endless scraped knees and elbows. He had a light step and a special sensitivity that Charlotte seemed to lack.

They often walked down to the dock and Charlotte described the brilliant fall colors for him.

"Most of the summer wildflowers are gone now," she said one day, as they ambled down the dirt road. "But I've never seen such beautiful colors on the leaves. Chicago was nothing like this! They are yellow and orange and fiery red. Oh I wish you could see them just once, Chris!"

Chris stopped and cocked his head, listening intently. "Listen to the trees whispering secrets to each other in the wind! Wouldn't you like to know what they're saying, Charli? What kind are they?" His sightless eyes lifted toward the blue sky.

"They are mostly birch and aspen. They are tall, skinny trees with their leaves way up high in the sky. The bark is white. The bark from the birch trees peels off like paper, but not the aspen." A few of the golden leaves floated down. She plucked one from her hair.

"Why, look!" she exclaimed suddenly, stooping down on the damp earth. "Here is one little bluebell that lasted through the cold September nights. It's shaped just like a tiny bell, so perfect. It's here all by itself beside the road. I wonder why the frost didn't kill it? Shall I pick it for you? Papa says it's all right to pick a flower every now and then, as long as we leave most of them in the woods."

"Oh no, let's not," said Chris. "It's managed to stay alive so long; let's not spoil it. Listen—there's a ship near the harbor."

They had reached the dock, where the clear autumn sunlight reflected off the blue-green water, turning it all to sparkles. Charlotte shielded the sun from her eyes with one hand. Sure enough, a ship was just coming into sight.

She looked at Chris, awestruck. "You were right! But how did you know? It's still so far away that I can't hear a thing!"

Chris sat down easily on the wooden planking, careful not to get slivers in his palms. He patted the space beside him. Charlotte dangled her legs over the edge, looking at him expectantly.

"Blind people sometimes have better hearing than those who can see. We have to learn to use our other senses to make up for the lack of vision. Mother counts on me to let her know when the bread is done baking because I can smell it long before she does."

Charlotte gazed at his peaceful face in admiration. "I had no idea," she breathed. "Chris, what is it like to be blind? You are the first blind person I've ever known, but you're not at all what I expected. You don't seem to mind it; you're always so happy."

"When we lived in London I went to a special school for blind children. They taught us how to look after ourselves, even though we can't see what's around us. Mama and Papa found another school like it in Boston. That's where I'll go this winter. I can read a special kind of print called Braille. It's made up of tiny raised dots in different patterns that make up words.

You learn to read the patterns, that's all."

Charlotte exclaimed, "How clever you are, Chris! I don't think I could do that."

"You learn to do what you have to do, Charli. I'm not always happy, though. Sometimes I long to be like you and Rob and Will. I wish I could see what you see: the great rolling waves of the lake, the blue sky, the stars at night. I wish I could see Mama's face." Tears welled up in his sightless eyes and he struggled to regain control.

Charlotte's hand closed tightly over his and she trembled. "I'm sorry Chris. I didn't mean to upset you. I'm always saying the wrong thing. Mama's told me a thousand times to think before I speak."

Chris shook himself and cleared his throat, patting her shoulder. "It's all right, Charli. I love you just the way you are. Sometimes I feel sorry for myself, is all. The ship is closer now!"

Charlotte jumped up. "Oh I can see it very well now! It's a fine ship—a wooden schooner with all its sails up! The sails are snapping in the wind and it's really clipping along. There are ladders made of rope that go from the deck all the way to the top of the mast. There are words painted on the side. Let's see... *You Tell*. That's a lovely name, isn't it? I wonder where it came from? It's probably headed for Washington

Harbor. There's a man on deck and he's waving!"

Charlotte waved frantically. "They saw us, all right!" she cried, her eyes shining. In a few minutes the ship disappeared from view. Charlotte heaved a great sigh. "Don't you wish you could be out there with them? I wish I were a boy so I could work on a big ship. Rob says he will someday." She sighed again.

"If you had your own ship what would you name it?" asked Chris.

Charlotte thought for a moment. "Something dashing like *Lake Superior Queen* or *Belle of the Ball*. If Mama had a ship she'd call it *Dead Calm*. She hates the sea—every time she gets in a boat she's seasick. What would you call yours?"

"I think I would call mine *Lady Charlotte*, after my favorite cousin," he said seriously.

"You silly," she answered, pleased. "Let's go back now. Mama and Aunt Cat are making chicken pie for supper. And we're having plum pudding for dessert!"

It was a sad day two weeks later when the company left. Charlotte had grown to love her cousin in those brief weeks. Tears rolled down her cheeks as she sat alone on the dock. Nothing was left of the departing ship but a wake that sent huge waves crashing against the dock.

Papa watched her from the trees and then came to her quietly. He stroked her hair softly and she leaned on his shoulder.

"It's hard to make new friends only to have to say good-bye so soon, isn't it, my little daughter?"

Charlotte nodded, too choked up to speak. Finally she cried out, "Oh Papa, why couldn't they stay? Couldn't Uncle Kent have worked with you at the mine?" She gazed at Papa with sorrowful eyes.

"Your uncle has a job waiting for him in Boston, Charli. And Chris needs the special school there. You want what's best for him, don't you?" he asked gently.

"I guess so," she whispered.

"You've a tender heart, Charli," said Papa. "But don't stop caring and loving because it hurts. There are people who sometimes enter our lives for a very short time and then leave again. Some of those people you will never think of again. But some of them change our lives forever in that very short time. I think that Chris was like that to you, wasn't he?"

Charlotte buried her face in Papa's flannel shirt and shook with sobs. He held her tightly and a tear rolled down his own cheek as he stroked her hair.

CHAPTER 13

SHIPWRECK!

WITH THE END OF OCTOBER came the end of sunny days. The days grew shorter, the sun hid behind dark clouds, and it was cold and wet. Papa got out of bed late at night to put more wood in the stove. Charlotte would hear the stove lid rattle and she snuggled more deeply under the heavy quilts, with only her nose peeping out in the icy air.

The last Saturday of the month, however, dawned clear and sunny. At the breakfast table Papa spoke eagerly. "With winter coming, Lake Superior will soon be too rough for travel. I've been wanting to visit Washington Harbor west of here before winter. There's a fishing cabin over there that we could spend the night in. Beth, what say you pack up some food for us and we'll have a little weekend vacation?"

William clapped his hands and ran circles around

the table. "Hooray! Hooray, we're going on a trip! Come on, Charli—let's go get ready!" He tugged at her braids in excitement.

Charlotte's heart beat rapidly as she packed her small bag. A trip on the lake in October! It was bound to be exciting.

Mama decided to stay home. She had been tired lately and would enjoy the quiet time alone. Robin couldn't be persuaded to miss his Saturday at the mine, so he and Mama waved good-bye from the front porch.

"Charli, you wear your mittens now, don't forget and tend to your brother. Make sure he wears his hat and..." her voice drifted off as they ran down the icy road.

The small boat, borrowed from Mr. Cadieu, glided up and down the large waves. Charlotte and William squealed in delight and held on tight. The wind was strong and Papa's full attention was given to managing the sails. It took several hours to reach Washington Harbor. On the way they passed Point Houghton, Cumberland Point, and Rainbow Cove. The ducks and loons had long since flown south, and wild Lake Superior was eerily silent.

Charlotte was thankful for her woolly hat and mittens. The wind had changed direction and become frigid and sharp. Dark clouds began rolling in from the northeast. Papa eyed them nervously.

"I don't much like being on the lake in this kind of weather! Mr. Cadieu warned me to watch out for this kind of sudden shift in conditions. Unless it blows over, we may have to beach the boat at Washington Harbor and find another way home!" He shouted to be heard over the wind and waves. Charlotte was silent. She wondered what other way there could be.

The waves in Washington Harbor rocked a large ship that was anchored near shore. Charlotte stared hard at it, thinking it looked somehow familiar. "It's the *You Tell*!" she cried. "That's the ship that Chris and I saw a few days ago!"

Papa nodded, his brows and beard now covered with snowflakes that began falling heavily. "They're probably waiting for the storm to blow over before they continue on to Duluth! I wouldn't want the job of keeping that ship afloat on a night like this!"

He made the boat fast to an old dock, tying knots in the ropes around iron cleats. The small log cabin was just a short walk away and they all breathed a sigh of relief when the door closed securely behind them.

Charlotte unwound her icy shawl and freed William of his coat and hood. The cabin was freezing, but Papa found a pile of dry wood under one of the bunks, and soon a fire burned steadily in the old cook stove. Charlotte dug into the food hamper and pulled out Mama's pot of stew. They drank cup after cup of hot tea with it, and ate half a loaf of Mama's good fresh bread.

"Now that's much better," said Papa with a worried sigh. He stretched out his long legs and lit his pipe. "Come, sit on my lap, Will, and listen to that wind howl! My we're in for a wild night tonight! The weather on Lake Superior changes faster than any place I've ever seen. If I'd guessed this morning that the day would turn out like this, I would have kept us all safe and sound at home!"

On Papa's lap, William whimpered. "I'm scared, Papa. Will this house blow away?"

"No, my son! This sturdy little cabin has withstood storms for many years."

William brightened. "Can we sing some songs? And then tell us a story?"

Papa's deep rich voice filled the tiny room with cheer. Charlotte and William marched about, slapping their hands and stomping their feet, until they flopped on the rag rug, exhausted, and thoroughly warmed-up.

They slept in their clothes, Papa in one bunk, Charlotte and William sharing the other. Charlotte had just fallen asleep, William's cold feet pressed firmly against her warm back, when a giant crash of thunder shook the cabin. "Papa!" she cried.

He put a finger to his lips. "Shhh, Charli. You'll wake Will. Come to the window, here with me. The storm is growing worse."

She pulled on her woolen socks and padded softly to Papa.

The storm had turned Washington Harbor into a rolling, churning beast. Great flashes of white lightening lit up the black sky, followed by deafening blasts of thunder. Dark, angry clouds chased each other across the sky. They piled up high, billowing up into towers and then suddenly falling apart when the wind tore through them. Enormous waves crashed against the shore, sending white spray far inland.

At that moment a great flash of light illuminated the harbor. Charlotte watched in fascinated horror as the *You Tell* struggled against the mighty waves. The large ship was taking on water badly. Muffled shouts from the crew on deck wafted to shore. When at last it looked as if she were winning the watery battle, a wave of terrific size crashed over the starboard deck. There was a terrible creaking wrench, and the ship broke in two. The great sails tumbled into the water with a tremendous splash. Wooden beams and planks crashed together in the frenzy of waves and wind.

Papa leaped into his boots and called to Charlotte, "Stay inside with Will. I've got to try and help those men get to shore!"

"No, Papa! Don't go! You might not come back!" She clutched at his coat sleeve, her eyes wide with fright.

"I have to, Charli," he repeated. "Those men are in trouble. I'll be back!" He pushed her inside and shut the door hard.

William had awakened. His small body trembled as he clung tightly to Charlotte's still form. Tears slid down her cheeks. She felt suddenly freezing and hugged William even harder.

The scene from the window was a nightmare. There was nothing left of the once-majestic *You Tell*. Her mighty sails were torn to shreds and littered the harbor with their tattered remains. Boards and planking, cracked and broken, tossed about blindly on the crests of rolling waves.

William trembled. "Where is Papa, Charli? Can you see him?" His teeth chattered when he spoke.

Charlotte pulled a heavy blanket around her shoulders and stepped outside. "It's too dark and now it's snowing! I can't see anything! Wait a minute—there's a row boat coming ashore and there are five, no six, men in it! I think Papa is the one rowing! Yes, it's him!" She hugged William tightly.

Papa was followed into the cabin by the five crew members. Shivering uncontrollably, they stripped off their soaked clothing. Charlotte found some wool blankets for them and put on a fresh kettle for tea.

She looked at the man they called "Captain." He was tall, with blond hair and skin that looked like old leather. She couldn't tell if he was young or old.

He peered out into the fury of the storm and sighed deeply. "She broke up before we even knew what was happening. Of all my years on the Great Lakes, I've never seen a storm blow up so fast. We're sure grateful to you, Mr. Avery. If you hadn't come along when you did, we'd be looking at the bottom of Lake Superior right now. Our life boat broke loose when she went down. Thank goodness we dropped off the last of our passengers last week."

He sipped the hot tea, his frozen fingers drawing heat from the mug. Charlotte spread out the wet clothing by the fire. Papa and the crew talked long into the night, their voices low and weary.

The morning dawned clear and bitterly cold. Charlotte scratched a peep hole in the frost on the window pane and squinted at the sunshine.

Papa came in as Charlotte was slicing the last of the

bread for breakfast. He was followed by two silent Indians. William's mouth dropped open and he stared at the dark men. They had often seen Indians around the village, but they had never been so close. They wore soft leather breeches and shirts and hats made of fur.

"Children," said Papa, "the storm really stirred up the lake in the night. The waves are too rough for our small boat to handle. We will have to hike back to Island Mine and leave the boat here until spring. These two men know the forest well and have agreed to lead us on foot back to Island Mine. Their names are Yellow Bird and Joe Take-A-Bite. They are spending the winter in a cabin near here. Joe and I met at the mine last summer. Was I glad to see him here this morning! Dress quickly and bundle up well. We have a long walk ahead of us today. How many miles would you say, Yellow Bird?"

"Twelve or fourteen miles. We know the way. You follow us."

"But Papa, what about the crew from the *You Tell*? They were gone when we woke up. Aren't they going back with us?" asked Charlotte.

"They are going to stay around here and try to do some salvaging. Don't think they'll have much luck, though. That storm ripped through everything in her path."

Joe and Yellow Bird led them through the forest. They walked on level ground at first, but soon there came a great ridge that seemed to go uphill for miles. The way was rough, and Papa carried William on his back until they reached the top. Joe said that was Sugar Mountain. Charlotte's legs were tired. Her toes and fingers were numb. She wished that she was a little girl again so that Papa could carry her, too.

When they reached a clearing, late in the afternoon, Papa brought out the bits of food that were left from the hamper. They stood in the snow and ate cold beans and cornbread. When it was all gone, Charlotte licked her fingers. She was still hungry. She saw a flash of gray high on the ridge, then a long, eerie howl broke the stillness. She knew this time that it wasn't a loon. She felt the hairs on the back of her neck prickle and stand up.

The small group huddled together, staring in the direction of the howl. Suddenly, from among the trees, stepped a large bush wolf. William screamed and Papa held him tightly to his chest. He slowly pulled Charlotte toward him, his eyes never leaving the wolf.

Yellow Bird put a finger to his lips. They stood motionless for what seemed like hours. Charlotte's knees trembled violently, but she didn't make a sound.

Her eyes were locked on the gaze of the wild creature.

He was the most beautiful, wild beast she had ever seen. His fur was thick and gray. His tail was full and bushy. It curled around his haunches, where he sat straight and tall. His pointed ears pricked up in alertness and his snout sniffed the wind. "He's smelling us," thought Charlotte. She felt a bolt of terror and excitement shoot up her spine. He opened his mouth to reveal rows of razor-sharp teeth.

When Charlotte thought that she could not remain still for one minute longer, the bush wolf stretched his front legs, then his back legs, and loped off into the forest.

Papa let out his breath in a rush. William and Charlotte scampered to the hill and stared at the tracks. The Indians remained silent.

They began to go downhill now. Everywhere they saw tracks made by deer and caribou and rabbits.

Charlotte grew so weary that she could barely make her legs go. Her feet were numb with cold and pain. The glare of the snow hurt her eyes. Every now and then Papa turned, giving her an encouraging smile. "Doing all right, Charli? Can't be much further now. That's my brave girl!" Charlotte tried to smile, but she could see worry in Papa's eyes, for the sun was low in the west and darkness began to settle in the forest. The moon shone eerily through the bare branches of tall maple trees.

When the last light faded from the sky, they came into an opening to see a log cabin ahead. It was Mrs. Cliff's boarding house. Then, they saw their own house.

Tears of relief welled up in Charlotte's eyes as they stepped onto the familiar patch of road. Mama burst through the door, the kerosene lamp she held casting a welcome glow on the white snow.

"Oh, thank God!" she cried, hugging them all at once. "Thank God! I was so worried, Ian. The storm was so terribly sudden, and the lake too rough to go and look for you!" She sobbed on Papa's shoulder. He spoke to her in low tones and dropped soft little kisses on top of her head.

Charlotte peeled off her heavy layers of clothing and stretched out in front of the fireplace. Her eyes closed immediately and she dreamed of the beautiful bush wolf.

CHAPTER 14

WILLIAM'S ACCIDENT

BY THE MIDDLE OF NOVEMBER, winter had descended on Isle Royale. Icicles hung from roofs, their jagged tips gleaming in the frosty sunshine. The air was crisp and there was finally enough snow to go sledding.

When Charlotte and William went outside to play they wore many layers on their feet. First came thick wool socks, then soft warm moccasins, and on top of everything, heavy boots. At school they removed the boots and padded about the schoolroom in the moccasins.

Recess was great fun in the cold weather. They breathed in deeply and the icy air stung their throats and nostrils. Mr. Adams, who ran the general store, saved the large round boxes that cheese came in, and Sara brought them to school. They were big enough to sit in and made wonderful sleds. The steep hill outside the schoolhouse was perfect for sledding. The children shrieked with laughter as the round boxes carried them down the hill. Every now and then someone would tumble out and get a face full of snow. But no one ever minded.

Charlotte and Claire liked to squeeze together into one large box and cling to each other in terrified glee as they careened downhill.

They tried for days to persuade William to try it, but he stubbornly refused. Then one sunny afternoon he gave in and scrunched down nervously beside Charlotte. After the first time his fear was gone. He went down alone, time after time, squealing with laughter.

"Did you see me that time, Charli?" he asked, his cheeks glowing from cold and exercise, his blue eyes sparkling.

"I sure did! You must be the fastest sledder I've ever seen!" She reached over and pulled his red-and-white muffler snugly around his neck.

He flashed a quick grin, grabbed the box, and raced up the hill to start again.

Claire examined something in the snow. "Look, Charli, tracks! I wonder what animal made them?"

Charlotte crouched down. "I think I saw tracks like

these before. I'll look it up in Papa's book tonight. Could be a moose, but..."

Her voice was drowned out by a shriek from the other side of the schoolhouse. The children dashed around the corner and peered down. A small figure lay at the bottom of the hill and beside it, an overturned cheesebox.

Charlotte screamed when she saw the red-and-white striped muffler.

"William!" she cried, lurching down the hill, tripping and tumbling through the snow. "William! Answer me, Will!" She turned him over. There was a vivid red patch in the snow and a deep gash on his white forehead. His eyes were closed and he didn't respond to her voice.

Claire was beside her, unwrapping her scarf. "Take this, Charlotte, and hold it on his head. We have to stop the bleeding!"

"Is he dead, Claire?" Charlotte barely whispered, the tears coursing down her cold cheeks. "Oh, it's all my fault! I should have been watching him! Why did I talk him into sledding? Didn't he know not to come down the side with all the trees? I'm not even sure I told him! Oh what will Mama say to me?" She held his head in her lap and rocked to and fro in the snow, not bothering to wipe off the icy tears that ran down her nose and chin.

Miss McKinney appeared at the top of the hill. "You big boys, pick him up gently and bring him to the schoolhouse. Careful, now! Don't jostle him any more than you have to."

Robin, eyes filled with shock and horror, picked up William's limp shoulders and another boy grabbed hold of his legs. At the top of the hill, Miss McKinney had stopped a passing bobsled. Gently they laid him in the bed of the wagonbox. Charlotte crept in beside him, clinging to his limp hands. The driver raced down the hill toward home.

Robin sat beside her, staring silently at William's still face. Charlotte sobbed, "Oh why doesn't he open his eyes? Why doesn't he wake up? It's all my fault!"

Robin looked at her sharply. "It's my fault as much as yours, Charli. I wasn't watching him either. Why did he go down that side of the hill anyway?" He rubbed furiously at his eyes and dropped his head.

Mama rushed out of the house as the wagon pulled up. "What's wrong! Why aren't you... and where is... oh my goodness!" She pulled William into her arms and stared straight ahead, her voice calm and controlled.

"Rob, run and fetch Papa at once! Charlotte, help me get him inside!"

Mama unwound the blood-soaked muffler and cleaned the wound with cool water. Still his eyes remained closed.

"This cut is deep. He will need stitches. There may be other injuries as well. Oh why did our only doctor have to leave?"

Charlotte wailed, "I'm sorry Mama! What if he dies? It's all my fault!" A fresh flood of tears erupted. Mama put her arms around her firmly.

"Chin up, Charlotte," she commanded in a stern tone. "Papa will have to take Will to Copper Harbor. That's where the nearest doctor is."

"But what about the ice in the bay? Papa said this morning that the bay was frozen over!"

"It's only surface ice, Charlotte. The boat will be able to break through the thin ice. Thank God that the supply boat is still in the harbor!"

Papa arrived. He examined William quietly and then, bundling the boy in warm blankets, carried him to the wagon.

"Rob, keep the fire going while we're gone. Don't forget to feed and water the horses, and be careful with the cook stove. Elizabeth, pack a bag quickly. The weather may keep us in Copper Harbor for several days. Charli, Rob is in charge—you do what he says."

Charlotte's eyes opened wide. "I have to come too,

Papa! I want to go! Please don't make me stay home! This was all my fault!" She fell into a crumpled heap at Papa's feet, her body racked with sobs.

Papa knelt beside her, gripping her shoulders tightly. "Charlotte, look at me. This was not your fault, and I won't hear you say that again. Will knew which side of that hill to play on. I talked to him about it myself. You can't be responsible for every choice he makes."

Charlotte clung to him, still weeping. "Please let me come, Papa. Please!"

He looked at her hard for a moment and then pulled her to her feet. "All right. You may come. But no more hysterics. Dry your tears and bundle up well. This is going to be a cold, rough ride."

The boat plowed swiftly through Siskiwit Bay. The ice made tiny tinkling sounds as the boat broke through.

Charlotte was quiet, exhausted from her tears. She held William's hand and looked at Mama. Mama's face was white and calm. The great waves of November rocked the boat mercilessly, but Mama wasn't seasick.

Night had fallen when they reached the dock at Copper Harbor. Papa carried William, while Mama banged furiously on the door to the doctor's office.

A small man with bushy black hair and spectacles

opened the door. Removing the pipe from his mouth, he beckoned them inside quickly. Papa laid William gently on the examining table, and the door was pulled shut wordlessly.

Charlotte trembled. The boat ride had been freezing, and her fingers and toes were numb. Papa put one arm around Mama and the other around Charlotte.

"We must pray now," he said. "If God wants Will to live, then it will be so." Charlotte gulped hard and buried her face in Papa's coat. It seemed like hours before the doctor returned, wiping his hands on a clean white cloth.

"I put in thirty-five stitches. He has a concussion. It must be quite bad for him to have remained unconscious for so long. We'll have to watch him tonight. By morning we'll know."

They took turns sitting with William through the long night. Charlotte laid down on the sofa, but sleep would not come.

Finally, the first rays of rosy sunlight shone through the eastern window over William's head. She watched his face intently. Suddenly she felt a feathery touch on her arm and she jerked. His eyes opened slowly and he looked at her sleepily.

"What happened to my sled? Hey, it was still my turn!"

Charlotte gasped and called to Mama and Papa.

"You little scamp!" Papa said, kneeling beside the bed. "You gave us quite a scare!" He fingered William's blond curls, tears of relief welling up in his tired eyes.

William lifted a hand and felt the thick bandage wrapped around his head.

"Hey, I've got a bandage just like Charli did when she broke her leg. Did I break my head? Let me see in the mirror!"

The tension in the room shattered and they all laughed uproariously.

That afternoon, Papa and Charlotte bundled up and went for a walk.

"It sure looks different in the winter, doesn't it, Papa?" she asked as they walked down Main Street.

"Indeed it does, my Charlotte." He stroked her long dark hair and continued. "Will's accident was a frightening experience for all of us. But the doctor says he'll be able to travel tomorrow. I am glad that you came along to help."

Charlotte smiled and reached for his mittened hand. The sun reflected off the new snow, nearly blinding in its pristine whiteness. They strolled along the rocky shoreline, stopping now and then to examine a trail of animal tracks. Ahead was a tree with a great hole bored into it. Small wood chips littered the snow beneath it.

"Look, Papa!" cried Charlotte, stooping down to finger the chips. "I'll bet this was made by a pileated woodpecker! I've seen one on Isle Royale; they're huge! No other woodpecker is large enough to have made a hole like this!"

Papa looked at her in admiration.

"You've turned into a real woods-woman since we came to Isle Royale, my little daughter. You really love it out here, don't you?"

Charlotte knew that her answer was important to him. She brushed the snow from a large slab of rock and sat down. "Oh, Papa," she sighed. "I do love it so! Claire is the best friend I've ever had. And there's Gram—she knows so much about trees and flowers and animals. And Miss McKinney—she makes me feel like I can do anything. You know what, Papa? She says that I have a talent for writing! I think I would like to be a writer when I grow up. Would that be good, Papa?"

"Charlotte, I think that would be wonderful. There has been some great writing done by women. But your Mama and I will be proud of you whatever you do. We are already proud of you." He looked far out over the ice-blue waves. "You are growing up, Charli. You have a ways to go yet, but already I can see it. You are a big help to Mama. She'll need your help even more in the next few months."

"Is something wrong with Mama?" she asked, alarmed.

"No, no, Mama's fine. But in the spring there will be another wee Avery in the house. Mama is going to have a baby," he finished softly.

Charlotte looked at him for a long time, not sure how to take the news. At last she spoke. "It could be a girl, couldn't it? I could have a sister!" Her gaze shifted to the lake and she jumped up. "I could have a sister!" She yelled this time, and did a jig on the rock.

Papa laughed. "Yes, it could be a girl, and it could also be a boy."

That sobered her for a moment, and then she grew cheerful again. "I think it will be a girl. It *has* to be a girl! What shall we name her, Papa? We could call her Emily, or Amy, or Molly is nice, don't you think? Oh, I can't wait to tell Claire!"

"You've got it all planned, don't you Charli-girl? But let's wait and see before we decide on names, all right?"

But Charlotte was too excited to slow down. "Oh, won't Claire be thrilled?"

Claire was indeed thrilled when Charlotte shared her news two days later.

"A sister would be lovely," she sighed. "But what if it's a boy, Charli? You'll have *three* brothers!" Her nose wrinkled in distaste.

"The baby will be a girl, I just know it. It will be jolly fun having a baby to take care of, won't it?"

Claire nodded, then looked slyly at Charlotte. "I have some news, too. I've just been bursting to tell you! Father is going to marry Miss McKinney! He told us just last night. I'm going to have a mother again!"

Charlotte stared at her in amazement. "I had no idea! I didn't even know they were courting! How absolutely perfect for you; she is such a dear! When will the wedding be—next spring?"

"That's the best part," Claire beamed. "They decided not to wait. It is to be two weeks from Saturday."

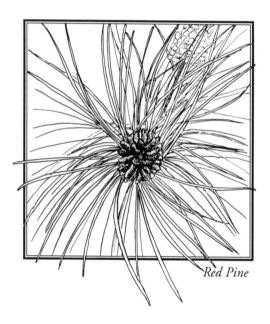

Red Pine

CHAPTER 15

THE WEDDING

MISS McKINNEY wouldn't hear of having the wedding indoors.

"But Shannon," Mama pleaded with her, "it's winter! How do you expect to have the ceremony outdoors? The guests will all get frostbite!"

Miss McKinney sat at the table in the friendly kitchen. She sipped her tea and set the dainty cup in its saucer. She looked at Mama, her eyes serious.

"Look around you, Beth. Have you ever seen such beauty as in this place? Oh, I dearly love my Ireland with its green valleys and rolling hills and cliffs overlooking the great ocean. But this island has quickly and completely worked its way into my heart. Getting married is the most important step I expect to take in my life. I want that step to take place where I can see the beauty that God created. If people can't tolerate the cold for a bit, then they needn't come. I've never been one to do things just to please others, and I don't intend to start now." Her mouth was set in that firm line that Charlotte had seen many times in school.

Charlotte turned sideways so she could see Mama's reaction. She was washing the lunch dishes. A few soapy bubbles slid onto the wood floor.

"Very well," said Mama with a sigh. "It's your day, you do as you like. But at least allow me to have a reception for you here. We have plenty of room."

Miss McKinney smiled. She placed her hand on Mama's. "That would be perfectly lovely. You are a dear for offering. You have been such a good friend to me."

Mama got up and began preparations in her head. "You just get your dress ready and leave the food to me. A potluck lunch would be nice, I think. Charlotte will be a help. We'll manage nicely."

Charlotte dried her hands and nodded eagerly. "And Claire and Gram can help, too! Gram makes the best cakes and pies."

News of the wedding spread quickly through the village. Social gatherings didn't happen often and were eagerly anticipated. Miss McKinney firmly declared her intention to keep teaching until the end of the term in the spring. Her decision was greeted with surprise. Married women just didn't teach school! But she was stubborn, and Claire's father supported her to the school board. There was no other teacher, so it was reluctantly settled that she would remain as teacher until June.

On the morning of the wedding, Charlotte awoke tingling with excitement. She had only ever been to one wedding, in Chicago. It was terribly stuffy and solemn. She was sure that this one would be quite different. Miss McKinney did things her way.

She hurriedly pulled on her Sunday dress and buttoned up with chilly fingers. It was a cold day, but the sky was clear and vivid blue.

Mama was in a hurried frenzy, running between kitchen and pantry and parlor.

"You'll have to get your own breakfast, Charli, and please see that Will eats, too. Don't slouch so, Rob! It isn't neat!"

Robin sighed. His high collar pinched his neck miserably. "Why do I have to go, Papa? Weddings are for girls!"

"You might feel differently about that some day, son," Papa chuckled. "We'd better be going. We're to help clear snow off the dock before the ceremony. Michael Cadieu will have his hands full with his new wife. She's bound to have her way, all right. A wedding outside on the first of December on Lake Superior! Whoever heard of such a thing?"

Mama pulled a comb through William's curls. "I've seen how Michael looks at her, Ian. He'd hand her the moon on a silver platter if she asked for it. And she thinks the world of him, too. They're well suited to each other. And it will be grand for Claire to have a mother."

Almost everyone in the village had risen early for the special occasion. They clustered in groups on the big dock, blowing on their hands and stomping their feet to keep warm.

Rays of pink and yellow sunlight streamed across the sky and reflected on the silvery ice in the harbor. Miss McKinney made her way slowly to the end of the dock, where her groom waited.

She had never looked lovelier. Her dress of creamy velvet hung in graceful folds from her slender waist. She wore a black velvet cape and matching hat. Her fiery red hair was piled high on her head, with a few wisps loose and curling around her face.

Claire's dress was blue silk, as was Gram's. Claire couldn't keep the happy grin from her face. Reverend Johnson spoke the familiar words and it was over quickly. Miss McKinney was pronounced Mrs.

Cadieu. She kissed her groom, then kissed Gram, then turning to Claire, kissed each of her cheeks tenderly. Claire beamed as she followed the bride and groom to the waiting bobsled.

Mama barked orders as she scurried between kitchen and dining room. Soon the guests began arriving, bearing hot dishes of food. The house filled up with people, young and old. Adults laughed and chatted. Teen-agers clustered by the fireplace. William and the other little boys dashed about merrily, lifting covers off pots, stealing cookies and candy. At last Mama caught him by the arm as he raced into the kitchen.

"William Henry Avery, every time I turn around, you've got something in your mouth. Lunch won't be for another hour, at least. Take your friends upstairs to your room and play quietly."

Charlotte watched him scamper up the stairs, wishing she could follow. But she was only halfway through the mountain of potatoes that Mama had told her to peel. How she hated to peel potatoes!

She ran the blade of the knife under a dark spot in the round potato. Then she felt a poke in her back. Claire was beside her, tying on an apron.

"I'll help, Charli! Wasn't it beautiful? Papa looks so handsome, and Miss McKinn... I mean, Mother, is beautiful, isn't she? Did you ever see so much food?"

The dining table was heaped with good things to eat. There were fresh loaves of bread: white and brown, and nutty-flavored graham bread. There were round cheeses and relishes and preserves in cut-glass dishes. There was baked ham and fried chicken and a huge stuffed turkey. There were large bowls of potatoes, mashed turnips, stewed tomatoes, baked beans, and squash. Then there was the dessert table. Charlotte eyed the sweets with longing. There were pies of all sorts: apple and raisin and mincemeat and pumpkin. And in the center of the table was an enormous platter heaped high with small white-frosted cakes.

The house was full and overflowing. At last the newlyweds blew in with a gust of swirling snowflakes. Mrs. Cadieu blushed prettily when the crowd began clapping. Papa stepped forward and held up a hand. The clapping and talking died down. He cleared his throat.

"Friends, guests, residents of Island Mine, let me introduce you to Mr. and Mrs. Michael Cadieu!" The clapping began again.

"Let me be the first to congratulate you, Michael and Shannon. May God bless you and may you have many happy years together! Now Reverend, if you would lead us in prayer, we'll enjoy this lunch that so many have worked hard to prepare."

Reverend Johnson stepped forward, bowed his head and began, "Lord, we thank you for this couple and for the marriage that has just taken place. We ask that you would grant them a lifetime of love and happiness together, and that their sorrows may be few. Bless this food to our bodies and thank you for the hands that prepared it. Amen."

Plates were filled and refilled. Late in the afternoon Claire and Charlotte washed dishes in the cluttered kitchen. "Isn't she wonderful?" sighed Claire. "It's so nice to call someone 'Mother' again! When Mama died, I didn't think Papa would ever find someone else."

Charlotte wiped a plate and set it in the cupboard. "What happened to your mama, Claire?"

Claire lifted her soapy hands from the dishwater. "I was only six when it happened," she answered slowly. "But I remember. Mama was going to have a baby. The baby came too early and Mama died giving birth." She looked into the dirty water and a single tear dropped into the bubbles.

"I'm sorry, Claire. I didn't mean to upset you!" whispered Charlotte, her cheeks burning. "I always say the wrong thing."

Claire picked up the dishrag and smiled. "It's all

right, Charli. I don't want to forget my mama. She had hair like mine and Gram's, and the loveliest voice. She would sing to me before I went to sleep. Songs about birds and flowers—the same ones that I hear Gram humming softly when she thinks no one's around. Gram misses her terribly, though she doesn't talk about it. Mama was her only child, you know."

"She sounds like a pretty special person," said Charlotte quietly. But she frowned. Mama Avery was pregnant. Suppose she lost her baby too? Or something happened to Mama? She shoved the thoughts from her mind.

In the evening when the last guest had gone, Papa, Mama, Gram, and the children sat wearily by the roaring fire. William slept, his small curly head resting on Papa's knee.

Charlotte and Claire lay on the wool rug, staring at the flames licking at white birch logs.

"Gram, tell us a story," begged Claire. "Tell us about when you and Gramps first came to Isle Royale."

Papa nodded. "That would be a treat, Margie. You know more about the history of Isle Royale than anyone else."

Gram chuckled. "What you mean, but are too kind

to say, is that I've been around longer than anyone else. But if you want to hear it, I don't mind telling it."

Charlotte propped herself up on one elbow and watched Gram's eyes sparkle in the firelight.

"As I've told you before, my Thomas and I came to Isle Royale back in 1834, when the American Fur Company opened up operations here. There were mostly Indians here then and only a handful of white men. That year we were part of a crew of thirty-three that came from Canada. They were coopers, voyageurs, fishermen, and managers. My Thomas, of course, was one of the fishermen. They set up centers at Belle Isle, Merrit's Isle, Grace Point, Duncan Bay, and Rock Harbor.

"We were at Rock Harbor mostly. Lived in a little log house that Thomas built himself. It had a roof of red cedar and was just as snug as could be. It was a happy life for us. Thomas was paid an annual salary of $225. The fishing crew went out every day in their Mackinac boats, powered by oars and sails, of course. They fished for lake trout, salmon, whitefish, and herring. My, I saw some beauties caught in those days!

"When they brought the fish in, they would hire some of the Indian women to clean and pack it in salt. The women took their pay in tobacco, pork, beans, or woolen socks. Every few weeks one of the forty-foot schooners came by to pick up the load of fish. What were the names of those boats, now?" She thought for a moment and then her eyes lit up.

"Oh yes. How could I forget? There was the *William Brewster* and the *Siskiwit*. It was always a big day when the boats arrived, same as it is today." She chuckled.

"What did you do for fun, Gram? Didn't you get lonesome?" asked Charlotte.

"Oh my, no, child. I had plenty to do. I had my little Kate, Claire's mama, to mind. We kept plenty busy. Sometimes we'd go and visit folks at the other fishing centers. We'd take a picnic along, pick berries, and work on sewing or mending. I don't recollect ever feeling lonely. But now I've rambled on long enough. Claire's heard all these stories before, but she always manages to talk me into telling them again." She tugged on Claire's hair-ribbons playfully.

"We've all had a long day. I'd better be getting this tired girl home to bed."

Mama and Charlotte walked with them to the door.

Upstairs, Charlotte yawned and paused at her bedroom door. "Mama, this day was the most fun ever. When I get married, I want it to be just like this."

Mama smiled and helped her into her nightdress.

"I thought you wanted to grow up and write books, little girl."

Charlotte thought for a moment. "Well, maybe I could do both. After all, Miss McKin... I mean Mrs. Cadieu is married now, but she's still a teacher."

"Yes, Charli, that's so. But it's late and you have years to decide. Right now just think about getting some rest." She tucked her in snugly and kissed her cheek. Charlotte was asleep before Mama closed the door behind her.

CHAPTER 16

WOLF AND QUEEN

WITH THE COMING of December, Isle Royale was struck with the full force of winter. Great drifts of snow covered the ground. Strong, frosty winds made the tops of birch and aspen trees sway to and fro. The sudden drop in temperature caused Siskiwit Bay to freeze over completely. No more boats would come and go until the spring thaw, months away.

But the residents of Island Mine were prepared for the months of ice-bound isolation. The shelves in the general store were crammed full of supplies. In the Avery home the cellar and pantry were brimming with good things to eat. Shelves were filled with Mama's good preserves, fruits and vegetables. There were bins overflowing with apples, potatoes, turnips, onions, pumpkins, and squash. In the shed behind the house hung hams and turkeys, sausage and venison, all wrapped carefully in heavy brown paper and frozen solid.

The walk to school through deep snow was difficult for William. Papa spoke of making a sled.

"If we had a pair of strong dogs, they could pull a sled all right. Charlie Murphy has a fine dog team. I believe I'll talk to him next time he comes about buying a couple of his pups."

Charlie Murphy delivered the mail between the mainland and Isle Royale. Since Lake Superior had frozen solid, Charlie drove his sled right across the ice. Charlotte loved to watch burly, heavily-bearded Mr. Murphy coming through the drifts with his team of strong, beautiful huskies. There were six dogs, all with glossy coats and bright healthy eyes. When their pink tongues lolled out of their mouths, it looked like they were smiling.

One day Charlie arrived with two extra dogs. Papa led them home on a stout rope.

"Come and see what I've got here!" he yelled from the back porch.

Charlotte whooped in delight when she saw them. She flung the door open and stepped out.

"Charlotte Anne Avery!" reprimanded Mama, "Put your coat on this instant! You know enough to do that without being told. Mercy on us!"

Charlotte flung her wool coat around her shoulders, William and Robin at her heels.

"Oh Papa, they're beautiful!" she cried, kneeling in the snow beside them. "Such fine, thick fur and bushy tails. Why, this one looks just like the bush wolf we saw in the woods that time!"

The large husky did look wolf-like. His bright eyes were narrow and slanted, his coat gray and white.

"Let's call him Wolf," suggested Robin.

Charlotte nodded happily.

"But what about the other one? What shall we name her?"

She was smaller than Wolf, with a quiet, gentle manner. Her tail thumped happily as William ran his fingers through her thick fur.

"She looks like a queen, all dressed in white," said William. "How about Queen?"

"They are already broken to harness, and I finished the sled last night. Who wants to go for a ride?" asked Papa.

Charlotte and William waited impatiently in the sled while Papa and Robin hooked up the harness. Mama brought out a string of bells and fastened them to the leather lead. "Now when I hear the bells jingling, I'll know where you two are," she said with a smile.

Charlotte and William hung on to the high sides of the sled as Wolf and Queen bounded happily through the snow. They worked together perfectly. When they went down Main Street, Charlotte waved at Sara Adams, who stood on the porch by her father's store.

"It's the most fun, Papa!" called William, panting for breath. "Now I don't mind going to school in the morning!" His cheeks were glowing with fresh air as he climbed from the sled.

For the first night Mama made Wolf and Queen a bed of blankets on the floor of Papa's office. "But after tonight, they sleep in the barn," she insisted.

That night, Charlotte awoke with a start. The bedroom was cold and dark. The small clock on the wall read twenty minutes past midnight. A sliver of moon laid a thin shaft of white light eerily across the polished wood floor.

What had awakened her? There was a noise. A dog barking? Yes, it came again—loud, frenzied barking from behind the closed door of Papa's office. She sprang from her bed and winced when her bare feet hit the chill floor. She pulled a shawl around her shoulders and went to the top of the stairs. Mama and Papa nearly ran into her in the darkness.

"I don't know, Ian," Mama was saying, behind him.

"Those dogs should be in the barn. Whatever could the matter be?"

Her words gave way to coughing. Smoke poured from the kitchen.

"Charlotte!" yelled Papa. "Run back upstairs and get Will and Rob. Go out to the barn and stay there until we come for you! Go now!"

He rushed into the kitchen through the thick smoke. Mama lurched to the office and freed the frantic dogs.

Fear tore at Charlotte's heart. She grabbed William's boots and shoved them on his feet. He rubbed his eyes and looked at her wearily. "What's wrong, Charli? I was having a good dream."

"Fire! Just like in Chicago! Oh what will we do if our house burns down?" she sobbed.

"Hush, Charli," said Robin quietly, pushing her down the stairs. "It isn't like Chicago. Papa knows what to do."

Robin tugged at Wolf and Queen's collars, leading them to the barn. In a few minutes Papa appeared. His eyes were red and he was coughing.

"It's all right, children. The fire is out. A log rolled out of the stove and started the floor to burning. The wood is scorched pretty well, but no great harm done."

Charlotte threw her arms fiercely around Wolf's

neck. "You saved us, Wolf, and you too, Queen," she whispered.

"Thank God for these dogs," said Mama softly. "And to think that we just got them today!" Tears sprang to her eyes.

Papa put his arms around her tightly. "Don't cry, Beth. Everything turned out all right, eh? And don't we have the two finest dogs on Isle Royale?"

After that day, Wolf and Queen were petted and pampered. Charlotte braided a special rag rug just for them. They slept on it in front of the fireplace.

On school mornings, Charlotte hitched them to the sled, and she and William rode in comfort. In the afternoon Mama sent the dogs back to school to bring them home.

The other children in school loved the beautiful dogs. They saved treats for them from their lunch pails—bits of meat or bread or half a cookie. Wolf and Queen accepted each gift politely with a tail wag and a grateful lick.

On sunny Saturday afternoons, Charlotte and William's friends came to the house to take turns riding the sled. When they got chilled, they went inside by the fireplace to eat bread and jam and drink hot tea. Charlotte loved those happy Saturdays.

CHAPTER 17

AN ISLAND CHRISTMAS

CHRISTMAS was just around the corner. School was to close for several weeks vacation. Mrs. Cadieu had planned a special day for all the village to attend.

"Children, let's talk about Christmas," she said in her musical voice. "What does it mean to you? I'd like to hear your thoughts."

Hands shot up throughout the schoolroom. Some thought of Christmas trees with candles burning brightly on green branches. Others thought of stockings hung by the fireplace, filled with treats. Some mentioned Father Christmas. William thought of only one thing. "Christmas candy, lots of it!"

"All those things are fun," said Mrs. Cadieu. "We all enjoy receiving gifts and treats at Christmas, and spending time with the ones we love. But there is so much more to Christmas. It is the time that we also think of what we can do for others. It is a time to show love and caring. I have an idea about a very special way that we can celebrate Christmas this year. I think we'll all enjoy it, and do something for others as well. Can anyone tell me what brought us all together to this village on Isle Royale?"

Claire's hand shot up. "Why, the copper mines, of course. Everyone who works here has something to do with the mine."

"That's right, Claire. Without the mines none of us would be here. Now let's think for a moment about the men that work in the mine. Many of them are just like us—from far-away countries, far from home.

"All of us have families to go home to at night. But most of the miners just go to the boarding house at the end of the day. Christmas should be a special time for them too, don't you think?

"I've spoken to some of the women in town. They are willing to prepare and serve Christmas dinner here at the school. Does anyone have other ideas for what we could do?"

Charlotte raised her hand. "Why don't we make a special gift for each of the men?"

"That was my idea exactly," said Mrs. Cadieu. "Now let me introduce you to a very special guest.

This is my friend, Cloud-In-The-Sky. She comes to us from the Indian camp nearby."

Cloud-In-The-Sky stood before them quietly. "My people live off the land, and we use what we find in the woods and waters. I have seen white men carry money in these things called wallets. Theirs are made of leather. I make them from birch bark." She held up a small white object. It was a beautiful piece of work, sewn intricately with precise stitches.

The children gathered round as she explained in her quiet voice how to shape and sew the soft bark. It was more difficult than it looked, the children discovered. Some of the wallets were a little awkward, but each one was made with love and care. In two weeks time, they had made enough of the little birch-bark wallets so that each of the miners could take one home.

On Christmas midday the Avery family all piled into the big sleigh. Mama had helped plan the meal. She was taking an enormous pan of chicken pie and a platter of crisp, fried donuts.

The schoolhouse was bursting with laughter and good will. The delicious dinner was enjoyed slowly, followed by Christmas carols and a short sermon.

Charlotte and Claire passed out the gaily-wrapped bundles to the miners. Mrs. Cadieu stood. "We just want to tell all you men how much we appreciate your hard work for the village. The children and I wish you a very happy Christmas." There was a great round of applause. They exclaimed over the clever gifts and carefully saved the wrappings. The evening ended with cups of eggnog and merry good-byes.

Charlotte sighed contentedly as she lay in bed that night. It had been a perfect Christmas. Mrs. Cadieu was right. Christmas *was* more than receiving gifts. Real Christmas joy came in bringing joy to others.

CHAPTER 18

Sugar Mountain

AFTER CHRISTMAS, the best days of winter seemed to be gone. It seemed as if it only just got light and the sun would begin to set. Charlotte felt anxious and restless. By the first of February she longed for the frigid winter to end—for the fresh spring breezes to blow through tender green leaves on the maple trees on Sugar Mountain. But spring was still months away. In the far north it crept in on slow, cautious feet, lagging far behind spring in places like Chicago and Detroit. Charlotte was staying indoors and helping with housework. She was tired of cold feet and runny noses and chilly baths in the kitchen washtub.

At last March arrived. One morning at breakfast Papa made an announcement.

"Sap is running in the maple trees on Sugar

Mountain. Yellow Bird and Joe Take-A-Bite spoke of it yesterday. They are busy as beavers making syrup. I've been wanting to visit the camp. Robin is working at the mine but how would you two like to go along with me this Saturday?" He looked steadily at Charlotte and William.

"Is it a real Indian camp, Papa?" asked William, biting into a piece of cornbread. A trickle of crumbs fell to the floor, where Queen licked them up. She never strayed from beneath William's chair at mealtime.

"Indeed it is, son. I'd like to do some trading while we're there—lay in our supply of maple syrup for the year. What do you say, Beth? Do you feel up to the walk?" He lifted her hand and pressed it to his cheek.

Mama sat down heavily. "I think I'll stay home, Ian. It would be too much for me. It doesn't take much to tire me these days. But you and the children should go. The outing will do them good."

William rested his cheek on Mama's expanding tummy. It wouldn't be too much longer before the new baby would be born.

"Very well, then," said Papa, pushing his chair back from the table. "We'll hitch up Wolf and Queen, and Charli and Will can ride in comfort."

Charlotte smiled at Papa. He always knew how to make her feel better.

The Indian camp was deep in the maple forest. Wolf and Queen pulled the sled uphill through mushy snow. Papa walked beside the sled. He wore snowshoes and carried a bundle of tobacco on his back to trade for maple syrup. Charlotte and William watched for tracks in the snow.

When they reached the camp, Yellow Bird came to meet them, his hand outstretched. "Fine dogs, Mr. Avery. You make good choice." He motioned for them to follow. Several women and children were eating from a large pot. A woman with long black braids and a soft leather dress handed each of them a bowl of stew. The warmth felt good on their cold hands.

William took a bite and wrinkled his nose. "What is it, Charli?" he whispered.

"I don't know. Some kind of wild animal, I guess. We mustn't be rude. Eat some more and stop grumbling." She took a tentative bite and swallowed it quickly.

"You like beaver stew, yes?" asked the woman. Charlotte and William looked at each other and gulped hard. The thought of eating one of those clever, furry creatures was too much to bear. When the Indian woman turned away, Charlotte quickly dumped what was left in their bowls back into the big pot.

"When it is time to gather sap in the spring," Yellow Bird explained, "our women come ahead while we finish hunting. They put up the wigwam. The vessels we use to hold the syrup are made of birch bark gathered last year." He picked up a birch-bark bucket and handed it to Charlotte.

She looked at the sewing carefully. It hadn't been sewn with ordinary thread. "This isn't thread," she said. "What do you use for sewing?"

"We use roots for sewing," said Yellow Bird. "They have to be sewn and sealed so that they won't leak."

"That is very clever," said William, his eyes serious.

Yellow Bird laughed. "Maybe you learn something from the Indians, little man?" He led them to a large maple tree. He made a gash in the tree about three and a half feet from the ground. Into the gash he forced a small cedar duct. He placed the birch bucket under the duct. Sap, clear and thin, dropped slowly into the bucket.

"Your syrup isn't like ours," said William. "Ours is thick and brown. Maple trees in Chicago must be different from Isle Royale trees."

Papa laughed. "You haven't heard the whole story yet, Will. There's more to it than this. Right, Yellow Bird?"

Yellow Bird led them to a large fire. Over the fire

hung an enormous vat.

"It's made of moose hide," he explained. "It holds about one hundred gallons." They watched as a young man tipped his bucket and poured clear sap into the vat.

"It cooks over a slow fire until it gets thick and dark. We save some of it for syrup. The rest of it keeps cooking until it gets hard and crumbly. That is maple sugar. We men keep the fire going. Children gather the sap. In the Indian camp, each person has a job."

As he spoke, he dipped a ladle into the boiling mass. He poured the thickening syrup onto a patch of clean snow.

Charlotte and William watched in fascination. The Indian children picked it up and popped it into their mouths. It was candy! A girl shyly offered them a piece. Delicious! Their eyes opened wide.

"You like Indian candy," Yellow Bird observed, smiling. They nodded eagerly.

Charlotte and William helped collect sap while Papa traded with Yellow Bird. In the late afternoon Papa loaded two great buckets of syrup onto the sled. He was happy to get the good syrup. Yellow Bird was happy to get new tools and plenty of tobacco. Charlotte and William walked beside the sled with Papa. Charlotte carried a small leather pouch with some candy in it for Mama and Robin.

"Papa," said Charlotte, stepping over a large rock in the path, "Mrs. Cadieu says that the Ojibway Indians came to Isle Royale long before white people. They even did mining for copper."

Papa rubbed his mittened hands together vigorously. "That's so, Charli. The pits that they dug are still visible in some areas. In fact, some of the current mining companies have begun exploration of the ancient pits."

"But Papa," she said puzzled, "if the Indians were here first, shouldn't Isle Royale belong to them?"

Papa was silent for several moments, lost in thought. At last he spoke.

"That's a good question, Charli. We owe a great deal to the Indians. They have shown the white man how to live successfully in the wilderness; they have taught us hunting and fishing, navigation of the lake, and which berries and plants are good for food. Without them we would be sunk.

"But I would say that this great, vast and lonely island really belongs to no one—Indian or white. Oh, I know the maps say it belongs to Michigan. But it really belongs only to itself and to mighty Lake Superior that surrounds it."

Charlotte walked quietly behind William, thinking about Papa's words.

When they arrived back at the house, Claire was sitting at the kitchen table, eating gingerbread. When she saw Charlotte, she jumped up.

"Guess what, Charli? Mother said that I might ask you to come and spend the night! Isn't it exciting?"

Charlotte's eyes pleaded with Mama. "Please, may I go, Mama? We've been wanting to do this for ever so long, and this is Saturday. No school tomorrow."

Mama looked doubtful. "I don't know, Charli. I really should keep you home. You only just get back from one outing to leave on another. It isn't proper for a young girl. And there's church tomorrow. You two will be up till all hours giggling and carrying on..."

Papa put an arm around Mama's waist and nuzzled her cheek. He spoke softly.

"Let her go, Beth. She's only young once. These experiences are good for her."

Mama sighed. "All right, Charli. Papa says you may go. I guess if you said you'd like the moon, he'd reach up and pull it down for you."

Charlotte did a happy jig. "Oh thank you, thank you! And I promise we won't be up all night."

"That's right, young lady. You be in bed by midnight. Promise me now. And no sleeping in church tomorrow."

Charlotte and Claire held hands as they dashed through the snow.

"'It will be such fun, Charli! And there's another surprise. Gram's brother is here for a visit! You'll love him. I'll get him to tell some stories—he's one of the last voyageurs, you know."

"What's a voyageur?" Charlotte asked, running to keep up. "I never heard of one."

"I'll let Uncle Frank tell you about it. He's a wonderful storyteller—almost as good as Gram."

"But how did he get here?" asked Charlotte. "The harbor is all frozen in."

"Didn't you know? The spring thaw has begun. An ice-breaker came in this morning, followed by the *Precarious*."

Blueberries

CHAPTER 19

THE VOYAGEURS

CHARLOTTE BARELY TOUCHED Gram's delicious dinner. She knew it was impolite to stare, but she couldn't take her eyes off Uncle Frank.

He was twenty years older than Gram, but looked as fit and healthy as someone half his age. The sun had baked his skin red-brown and etched deep lines around his eyes and mouth. He stood no taller than Charlotte, but his thick arms and legs were powerfully muscled.

After washing the dishes, they gathered round the fireplace. Mr. Cadieu popped corn and they drank big mugs of cool cider.

Claire sat on Uncle Frank's knee. "Tell us a story, please! Charlotte has never heard of the voyageurs."

"Never heard of the voyageurs, you say? My, what do they teach them in school these days?" He winked at Mrs. Cadieu. "You've heard all my stories, little Claire. I'll put everyone to sleep."

"Come now, Frank, stop teasing. You know there isn't a soul around who can resist your stories." Gram rocked and knitted, her needles flashing in the firelight.

"All right then, Charlotte Avery. I guess you're stuck. There aren't many left now to tell how it was, so I guess it's up to me to pass it on.

"I'm no young man, as you can plainly see. I was born way back in the year 1790. My father and his father before him were voyageurs. They were French-Canadian.

"Well, in Europe there was a great demand for furs: otter, lynx, marten, and especially beaver. They were used for making fancy clothes and hats. Indians had plenty of those furs, but they wanted the white man's tools, blankets, tobacco, and such. So trading began.

"The Hudson's Bay Company was founded in 1670, and monopolized the trading industry. Then in 1784, all of a hundred years later, the North West Company was started in Montreal. My father worked for that company, same as I did."

He paused for a swig of cider. Charlotte asked, "So the voyageurs trapped animals for their fur and then traded with the Indians?"

"No, child. Not at all. The Indians trapped animals for furs. The job of the voyageurs was entirely different. Some voyageurs traded for furs from the Indians and transported them from the region west of Lake Superior to a stockade called Grand Portage in Minnesota, just a few miles from here.

"My run with the other voyageurs was between Montreal (that's in eastern Canada, mind you) clear across Lake Superior to Grand Portage. We traveled across the Great Lakes in four-hundred-pound canoes made of birch bark. They were long and wide and could hold thousands of pounds of trade goods or furs. We paddled for months at a stretch to get those furs from Grand Portage and bring them back to Montreal.

"As you know, Lake Superior isn't always easy to navigate, especially from the seat of a canoe. There were long days and sometimes not much rest. But it was a good life—the best life for those young and strong and adventurous."

Charlotte was round-eyed. "Whatever did you eat?" she asked.

"Well, nothing like my little sister fixed for dinner here tonight, that's for sure!" he chuckled. "We mainly lived on pea soup or corn mush, and the western voyageurs ate buffalo pemmican."

"What's pemmican? It sounds funny."

"They learned from the Indians to make pemmican; it's very rich in energy. If there wasn't buffalo meat, they used moose or caribou. It was dried and pounded fine. Then the dried powdered meat was mixed with lard. It was packed into sacks weighing about ninety pounds apiece. The voyageurs from the western plains generally ate that twice a day. After a few weeks of pemmican, they were mighty glad to get to rendezvous at Grand Portage—and so were we! There we'd get fresh fish or meat and vegetables.

"Sometimes the weather was too rough to paddle. On those days we had time to hunt for wild berries; those were sure a treat!"

"Tell about rendezvous, Uncle Frank," urged Claire.

"I was getting to that. When we reached Hat Point (the French call it *Pointe Aux Chapeux*), near Grand Portage, we'd go ashore and clean up. Oh we turned into a dandy lot then! We'd doff our old, dirty clothes and change into clean britches and shirts, put on jaunty hats and bright scarves. Then we'd make our grand entrance into the harbor.

"But the work wasn't over when we reached the shore. Not by a long shot. Do you know what a *portage* is, Charlotte?"

Charlotte shook her head, a handful of popcorn

forgotten in her lap.

"A portage is what you do with your canoe and supplies when they have to be carried from one body of water to another over land. Our bundles of trade goods from Montreal had to get to the Pigeon River, but from Grand Portage the only way was by land. The rapids on the northern stretch of the river were quite impossible to navigate.

"That portage was nine miles long! We usually carried two of those ninety-pound bundles on our backs. I knew a few men who could carry even more. Only when the portage was finished could we finally relax for a spell.

"At rendezvous there was great feasting and storytelling and much merrymaking. But after rendezvous we feared an early freeze-up of waterways in the late autumn, so we'd start out again soon on the 1,200-mile trip back to Montreal.

"Yes, those were fine days. Hard, back-breaking work. But that's why God gave us strong backs, eh? Those days are gone now; voyageurs have been replaced by the large boats on the Great Lakes."

Mrs. Cadieu had been silent throughout Uncle Frank's story. She looked at him earnestly.

"That is the most incredible tale I've ever heard! And to think that it all happened here! These stories must be preserved. Frank, won't you come and tell all the schoolchildren about the voyageurs? They would be fascinated."

Uncle Frank blushed. "I've never spoken to a whole group before, but I guess I could give it a try for you, Shannon."

He was as good as his word. Before departing in late April, he visited the school and shared his wonderful experiences with the young, wide-eyed audience.

When it was time for him to leave, the whole village congregated at the dock to bid him farewell. They had grown to love this man who had lived a fascinating piece of northern history.

"Why do people always have to leave?" asked Charlotte sadly, as Uncle Frank's boat left the dock.

"It's the way life is, little Charli," answered Papa. "The only thing that's certain in life is that everything changes."

CHAPTER 20

New Arrival

IT WAS LATE THAT NIGHT that Charlotte jerked awake. The bedroom was pitch black. Not even a glimmer of moonlight fell through the thin curtains. She lay quietly listening under the quilt. What had awakened her? Could there be another fire? But no—Papa had fixed the stove door. The dogs weren't barking, either. Then she heard a door open and close. Papa's heavy footsteps stopped at the boys' room. There were low voices, but she couldn't hear the words.

Papa opened her door, holding the lamp in front of him. The light revealed worry in his eyes. Charlotte propped herself up on one elbow.

"What's wrong, Papa? Where's Mama? Has something bad happened?" She sat up and threw the covers off.

Papa knelt beside her. "Your mama's time has come,

Charli. She needs help. Rob's gone to fetch Gram and Mrs. Cadieu. I need you to be with William. He does not understand, and he's upset."

Charlotte's eyes opened wide. "But Papa, it isn't time yet. Mama said the baby wouldn't be born until the end of May."

"That's what we thought, Charli. But it appears that your new brother or sister has different ideas." He attempted a smile.

"Oh Papa, Claire's mother died when she had a baby that came early. Is Mama going to die?"

"No, Charli. Mama will be fine; I'm sure of it. Now be a brave girl and go to Will. Gram has delivered hundreds of babies in her lifetime. She will know just what to do." Papa sounded like he was trying to convince himself that his words were true.

William sat on his bed wrapped in blankets. He was frightened. "Charli! Where did Rob go? Why is everybody up? Why won't Papa let me see Mama?" He wailed the last words and Charlotte drew him close. She was a big girl, she reminded herself. But she could not stop her tears from mingling with William's.

There were voices downstairs. Gram and Mrs. Cadieu went in to Mama and shut the door behind them.

Later downstairs, Papa put the kettle on and he and Robin stood by the stove, their hands warming around mugs of hot tea. Charlotte cut a loaf of bread and buttered a slice for William. He nibbled it quietly. They stared at each other, eyes wide and weary. At last Papa broke the silence.

"Come, Rob, let's make a fire in the fireplace. This kitchen doesn't seem to want to heat up tonight."

The warmth of the crackling fire was comforting. They sat close to Papa, drawing strength from each other.

He looked at each of them quietly. "I sometimes think that we fathers have everything backward. We worry and fret about money and jobs and getting ahead all day long—all our lives long. When all the time it's our families that really bring us joy. I want you three to know that I am very privileged to be your father. Nothing in life means more to me than knowing that my children are growing up to be fine people." He looked at Robin.

"My oldest son. You will soon be a man. Already you stand as tall as me! You have earned a reputation at the mine as a good, honest, dependable worker. You also help with chores without grumbling anymore. I'm proud of you, Rob." Robin blushed and looked at the floor.

"And you, my little man," he said to William. "You are growing too! You have done well in your very first year of school. And I can always count on you to make sure that Wolf and Queen are fed and watered. I'm proud of you, Will." William buried his face in Papa's shirt.

"And my Charli," Papa said finally. "You have blossomed into a fine young lady in the past year. My little city girl has learned to love the woods. You know more about flowers and birds than I do. You've also learned to be a good cook and a wonderful little mother to Will. I'm proud of you, daughter."

Charlotte wrapped her arms around Papa's neck. How she loved him!

A cry came from the bedroom upstairs and Papa sprang to his feet. Gram peered down the stairs.

"It's all right! Everything is fine! Papa may come up first." Papa dashed up the stairs, two at a time.

"Gram didn't say if it was a boy or a girl," said Charlotte, puzzled.

William proclaimed loudly, "I'm sure it's a boy, right Rob? No more sisters!"

Mrs. Cadieu beckoned to them. "Your mama is fine now, but she had a rough time of it. So go in quietly." They crept in soberly. Papa sat on the edge of the bed, holding Mama's hand. Mama smiled and held out her arms. On the pillow beside her, a tiny bundle squirmed.

"Children, let me introduce you to your new brother, Lyle."

Robin and William beamed. Charlotte's face fell. She blinked hard to keep the tears back. She had so longed for a sister. She reached out and stroked Lyle's downy cheek.

Then from a dark corner of the room, Gram stepped forward. She laid a wiggling bundle in Charlotte's arms. Her eyes flew open wide.

"*Two* babies? Mama, you had two babies... twins! Oh my goodness, you didn't know before, did you?" And then she stopped. "Is it? Could it be...?"

Mama's smile broadened. "And Charlotte, meet your very own sister, Laura."

Charlotte's eyes filled with fresh tears. "A sister of my very own," she whispered. She stroked Laura's soft brown hair in wonder. "They are both so perfect, and so tiny!"

"They're small, all right," said Gram. But they're healthy. They'll do fine, I should think."

William only stared. "Mama grew two babies at once," he said in awe. "She must be the most clever mama in all of America."

They burst into laughter. Papa swung William in

the air. "At least we've still got the women in this family outnumbered, don't we, son?"

Charlotte lingered for a few minutes after the boys left. She gazed in wonder at the twins, marveling at their perfect tiny fingers and toes.

Mama patted the bed. "Sit down, Charlotte." She brushed a long strand of hair back from Charlotte's face. "Can you manage the meals for the next couple of days? It will be a lot of work for you, I know. But we can't ask Gram to stay too long."

Charlotte patted Mama's hand. "Don't worry, Mama. I can manage fine! Claire will come and help. You just rest."

Mama laid back on the pillows and closed her eyes. "I *am* tired. You are a good girl, Charli. We're going to have our hands full with two babies to care for, aren't we? But I know I can count on you to help out."

"Of course, Mama. I remember lots about taking care of babies from when Will was born. It will be fun." She got up. "I love you, Mama. And you too, little Lyle and Laura." She planted a light kiss on each pink cheek.

When the breakfast dishes were washed, Charlotte pulled on her coat and stepped into her shoes.

"Papa," she called, "I'm going to run over and see Claire for a minute. I'll be back to see to the laundry in a bit."

"No need for such a rush, Charli. I know you two will want to visit. We men can hold down the fort for awhile."

Charlotte raced down the slushy road. When she rounded the bend she nearly plowed into Claire. They looked at each other and burst into laughter. Claire scraped mud from her shoes with a stick.

"Papa wouldn't let me come see you until after breakfast. What is it? Wait, let me guess! I don't need to guess. From the look on your face, I think you got your sister!"

Charlotte clasped her hands. "You're right! They named her Laura, isn't that lovely? And her hair is the same color as mine! But guess what? Laura came with a brother! Mama had twins! The boy looks just like Will, curly hair and all. Can you believe it?"

Claire gave Charlotte a mighty hug. "I'm so happy for you, Charli! I saved some pennies from Christmas. Let's buy candy to celebrate!"

CHAPTER 21

LEAVING ISLE ROYALE

THE EARLY DAYS OF JUNE came with wel-comed sunshine and gentle breezes. There was just one more week of school before summer vacation.

Mama was busy from morning till night caring for the twins. There were endless diapers to change, baths to give, and tiny clothes to launder. Every day Charlotte hurried home from school to help. She loved the twins dearly, and never tired of rocking them gently to sleep.

Mama insisted that Charlotte be free on Saturdays. She and Claire spent pleasant afternoons exploring the forest, making cookies with Gram, or sitting on the big dock and watching gulls, loons, mergansers, and golden-eyes.

The last day of school was a sad one for Charlotte. She had grown to love dear Mrs. Cadieu. In the fall a new teacher would come to Island Mine. Charlotte came to her as she wiped off the blackboard.

"Mrs. Cadieu?" she said shyly, "I just wanted to say thank you for helping me and for being a good teacher. I know I'll still see you, but it won't be the same."

Mrs. Cadieu dusted off her hands and looked out the window. "No, it won't be quite the same, will it? I shall miss my teaching. But, Charlotte, everything always changes in life. You can count on that. Change isn't always bad, though. It shakes us up a bit, and forces us to explore new directions. It helps us to grow into richer, stronger, more interesting people.

"I think we both have a bright future ahead of us! I have a daughter and husband to look after, and you have your whole life ahead of you!" She sat at a desk and pulled Charlotte down beside her.

"You have a clever mind, Charlotte. But even more importantly, you have a kind and caring heart. We live in an age when certain roles are expected of women. But I believe we can change that! Oh, I believe with my whole heart in being a wife and mother, but I also believe that there's more for us out there! Perhaps you will be one to look further and do great things. If you want to see the world, go see it! If you want to be a writer, start now! I believe in you, Charlotte. I know that you will grow up and make a difference."

At the dinner table that night, Mama and Papa were unusually quiet. Charlotte looked from one solemn face to the other. Neither spoke until Mama served dessert.

"Children," said Papa. "There is something we need to discuss. Several weeks ago Mama and I received a letter from my father in England."

Charlotte's eyes opened wide. Papa seldom spoke of his family. She had never met Grandma and Grandpa Avery.

"It seems," continued Papa, "that his health is poor. His business is failing, and he has asked for my help. Mama and I have thought long and hard about this. As you know, there have been troubles between my father and me. We haven't always seen eye to eye on many matters. But it is unsure how much longer he will live. Apparently, he is sorry for many things he said to me when Mama and I were married. Now he is longing to meet his grandchildren." Papa toyed with his fork, his pudding cold and forgotten. He took a deep breath.

"I don't know if I'm ready yet to forgive my father, but for the sake of all of you, I won't be much of a husband and father unless I try." Mama smiled and took his hand.

He continued, "I've written and told him to expect

us within the next three months. We're going to England!"

Charlotte's face drained of color. She jumped up from the table. Her glass tipped, spilling milk on the tablecloth and floor. She stared at Papa wordlessly, then fled upstairs.

She lay on her bed, tears soaking the pillow. Papa came and sat down beside her, stroking her hair. He said nothing for a long time. When her sobs tapered off, he turned her face to him gently. Charlotte was surprised to see tears rolling down his cheeks.

She whispered hoarsely, "Why, Papa, why? We are all so happy here. And Claire is the best friend I ever..." She choked and fresh tears fell on the bedspread.

"I know it's hard, Charli. Really I do. It was a terribly hard decision for me to make. But you knew when we came to Isle Royale that this wouldn't last forever. The mine is well established now, and my job here would soon be finished anyway."

Charlotte wiped her eyes sadly. "Why do you have to help your father now, when he never cared about any of us before?"

Papa cleared his throat. "I know it's hard to understand. And now isn't the time to explain it all. Some day I will tell you the whole story. But for now just try to bear it for me, eh? I would never do anything deliberately to hurt you, Charli. You know that, don't you?"

Charlotte nodded wordlessly and flung her arms around him. "It will be hard, especially leaving Claire. But I will try to be a brave girl." She thought of Mrs. Cadieu's words just that morning. This would be another step for her in the changing, growing process of becoming an adult.

Papa rubbed her back. "I've hired some people to do the packing and cleaning. Mama and I want you to be able to spend the month that we have left here with Claire. You will like England, Charli. London is a wonderfully exciting city with so much happening. And you have cousins there, you know."

Charlotte's and Claire's time together was precious. They spent long days talking and walking and promising to write letters often.

"You know," said Charlotte, the day before they would leave, "I've loved each placed I've lived so far. Chicago was fine. Isle Royale has been wonderful, especially meeting you." She squeezed Claire's hand. "Maybe I'll love London, too. Papa does, and so does Mama. And your father said that you might come for a visit some time." She looked at Claire hopefully.

"Yes, that's so. I believe you can find beauty wherever you live, like Mother says. I would love to visit you in London! But Gram would never be content to leave Isle Royale. And maybe I wouldn't either. This place has a way of gripping hold of your heart and hanging on tight. Do you know what I mean?"

Charlotte laid back and looked at the blue sky. She did know.

Claire, Gram, Shannon, and Michael Cadieu were on the dock to say good-bye the next day. The *Precarious* had been loaded the day before. She had received a fresh coat of paint and gleamed white in the early morning sunshine.

Charlotte stood on the wide deck, trying hard to keep the fountain of tears from springing forth again. Papa put his arm comfortingly around her shoulders.

Claire darted into the woods. The crew's strong arms released one rope from the dock. Charlotte looked earnestly for Claire who reappeared breathless, and reached an arm up to Charlotte.

Charlotte clasped her hands and something thin and fragile was slipped into hers. Claire backed up as the last ropes were untied. There were shouts and waves and farewells.

Charlotte swallowed hard and wiped away one tear as it threatened to fall. She watched the water below and the sky above. Her hands were clinched tightly at her sides. She watched the dock until it disappeared from view.

As the boat entered the open water of Lake Superior, a loon called out its wild and lonely and haunting song. Charlotte unclasped her hands. In her palm was Claire's last-minute gift. It was a tiny, perfect fairy slipper—her "friendship flower"—beautiful and delicate, like the friendship it represented. Charlotte pressed it to her cheek and breathed in deeply of Lake Superior's pure air.

A Note About Writing *Charlotte Avery*

Rebecca Curtis researched and wrote most of this story while working on Isle Royale in the summer of 1994. However, her love and knowledge of the island grew initially from several backpacking trips on the island and working there an earlier summer during college.

Ms. Curtis based much of her story on a published interview with Kate Eliza Knowles who was a young girl on Isle Royale in the 1870s. The interview appeared June of 1939 in the Houghton newspaper called the *Daily Mining Gazette*. She also found many other resources such as the journals of Sarah Barr Christian who lived on Isle Royale as an adult in the 1870s and another diary which describes traveling on the Great Lakes in 1874.

Many events in this book are based on true historical accounts. The story of Charlie and Angelique Mott, the wreck of the *You Tell*, the American Fur Company's history on Isle Royale, the account of the fur trade voyageurs, the description of mining operations, and the layout of the village of Island Mine are all factual.

Also, the description of how people lived on the island during this period is accurate. For instance, types of foods eaten and how they were stored, children using cheese boxes for sleds, and winter mail delivery by dog sled were details found in historical accounts of the time.

A Note About Isle Royale Ecology

Isle Royale became a National Park in 1931. Since it is now a wilderness area, primarily accessible by backpacking, there is a policy which prohibits picking any flowers and plants.

Wolves are first known to have come to Isle Royale in 1948. Prior to that time, early pioneers on the island recorded spotting "bush wolves" which were probably coyotes. Recent studies of the wolf population and its relationship to moose on the island have made Isle Royale widely known.

Isle Royale Resources

Isle Royale National Park (headquarters)
800 E. Lakeshore Dr.   Houghton, MI 49931
Phone: 906/482-0984

For information on transportation to the island, lodging, camping, and visitor information packets.

Isle Royale Natural History Association
800 E. Lakeshore Dr.   Houghton, MI 49931
Phone: 906/482-7860

Publications on Isle Royale natural history and cultural heritage.

Recommended Books

Once Upon an Isle: The Story of Fishing Families on Isle Royale
Paintings and Companion Stories by Howard Sivertson, Wisconsin Folk Museum, 1992. History of family fishing heritage on Isle Royale in the 1930s told with 40 colorful paintings and delightful stories.

The Illustrated Voyageur
Paintings and Companion Stories by Howard Sivertson, Midwest Traditions, Inc., 1994. Story of the life of the fur trade canoemen of the north told with 31 action-filled paintings.

Borealis: An Isle Royale Potpourri
Tim Cochrane, editor, Isle Royale Natural History Association, 1992. Collection of seven essays about cultural history of the island including logging, mining, and the resort era.

Paddle-to-the-Sea
Holling Clancy Holling, Houghton Mifflin Co., 1941. Classic children's tale of the journey of a carved canoe through the Great Lakes. Beautifully illustrated Caldecott Award winner.